THE HUNTERS

JOHN LaCASSE

SUNBURY PRESS
Mechanicsburg, PA USA

Published by Sunbury Press, Inc.
Mechanicsburg, Pennsylvania

www.sunburypress.com

Copyright © 2025 by John LaCasse.
Cover Copyright © 2025 by Sunbury Press, Inc.

Sunbury Press supports copyright. Copyright fuels creativity, encourages diverse voices, promotes free speech, and creates a vibrant culture. Thank you for buying an authorized edition of this book and for complying with copyright laws by not reproducing, scanning, or distributing any part of it in any form without permission. You are supporting writers and allowing Sunbury Press to continue to publish books for every reader. For information contact Sunbury Press, Inc., Subsidiary Rights Dept., PO Box 548, Boiling Springs, PA 17007 USA or legal@sunburypress.com.

For information about special discounts for bulk purchases, please contact Sunbury Press Orders Dept. at (855) 338-8359 or orders@sunburypress.com.

To request one of our authors for speaking engagements or book signings, please contact Sunbury Press Publicity Dept. at publicity@sunburypress.com.

FIRST SUNBURY PRESS EDITION: July 2025

Set in Adobe Garamond | Interior design by Crystal Devine | Cover by Lawrence Knorr | Edited by Barbara Kindness.

Publisher's Cataloging-in-Publication Data
Names: LaCasse, John, author.
Title: The hunters / John LaCasse.
Description: First trade paperback edition. | Mechanicsburg, PA : Sunbury Press, 2025.
Summary: John LaCasse's series journeys through danger, desire, and defiance, culminating in *The Hunters*—a breathtaking finale where resilience triumphs and justice ascends. This climactic chapter transforms survival into legacy, offering readers an unforgettable resolution woven with purpose and power.
Identifiers: ISBN : 979-8-88819-322-8 (paperback).
Subjects: BODY, MIND & SPIRIT / New Thought | BODY, MIND & SPIRIT / Shamanism | BODY, MIND & SPIRIT / Afterlife & Reincarnation.

Designed in the USA
0 1 1 2 3 5 8 13 21 34 55

For the Love of Books!

To The Penrose Triangle.

For all those who walk in outside dimensions.

Author's Note

The Hunters, third book of the *Deals, Danger, Destiny, Floppy Feathers* series, is not a history of religion. It is not an investigation of religious scandal. It is not a book about astrophysics or metaphysics. It is my lived experience with three women who by any measure are light beam riders.

Jacqueline, Kelly Marie, and Princess Merrilee are astounding women with extraordinary talent. There is love and trust, anger, and compassion. Each woman has a specific talent suited to the story. Two of them: Jacqueline and Kelly Marie, are from Earth (Canada and the United States). The other, Princess Merrilee, is from NGC-234 and M31, or 2.5 million light years away.

I am reminded of Roger Penrose, English philosopher of science and Nobel Laureate in Physics, and his *Fashion, Faith and Fantasy in the New Physics of the Universe*. (Princeton University Press). Never do Jacqueline, Kelly Marie or Princess Merrilee disregard the prospect that truth is only a matter of time. And those who fly in faith and fantasy are advancing the facts.

The extraordinary station in *The Hunters* is how two women come together to help a starseed search the cosmos for the Higher Order of God. Jacqueline, the leader with a chief executive (CEO) background. Kelly Marie, an outside-the-wire academic. Princess Merrilee, the starseed protagonist, with mind-bending capacity and power.

In their travels, they manage to round up some of the biggest names in history, not least The Scorpion of the Zodiac. Thomas Aquinas, medieval scholastic. Che Guevara, Cuban Revolutionary. Solomon, as in King

Solomon. Muhammad, Prophet of Islam. Hildegard of Bingen, Patron of Musicians and Writers, and Sun Tzu, famous for *The Art of War*.

In the pages that follow, we looked for answers. Some are circumspect. All transform the ordinary into the extraordinary. We bested the speed of light and danced with the revelations of existence in a unique and daring chance.

John

Jacqueline turns to John, "Did you ever know you were some kind of doppelganger Devil?"

"No . . . well, maybe. There were times when my thoughts and my actions didn't seem to fit a normal human system architecture. Like I was 500,000 copies of myself, and I was lost trying to select the path to an outcome.

"When I made decisions" . . .

"Wait a minute, John! Who is talking right now, you or Lucifer?"

Jacqueline was surfacing with her management style.

"I don't know, Jacqueline. As I see you looking at me—asking me these questions—I fully understand you are a flawed personality with a narrow range of understanding. I know you hate me, and I do not care because I dwarf you and all you represent."

Che Guevara leans into Hildegard of Bingen with "Doesn't sound much like John to me."

They both laugh.

Mount Olympus was still standing in the background. The mental suspension of reality was hovering over everyone. Merrilee was about to move all this "Most High" concurrency back to data. The whole *Mount Olympus and walk with the gods* sequence was going to disappear into qubits. No distinct matches for reference. No handouts of the experience. Nothing machine-readable. Just electromagnetic fuzz.

With the Milky Way galaxy self-destructing under the anger of Mars—the crush of the Zodiac and the death of Scorpius only hours before—then a thirty-three hour deep space trip to Mount Olympus where Starseed Merrilee gets the "I walk with the gods" nod from Thor, this group has become the Quantum Enigma of all time. And now, they have the added problem of John. Or Lucifer, Or the Devil—or not. Jacqueline instinctively knows John is speaking as the Devil. She laughs.

Kelly Marie turns to Merrilee. *"Wouldn't this be better if you just told us what's going on here?"*

All the nodding heads seemed to agree. Saint Thomas Aquinas, Hildegard of Bingen, Che Guevara, Sun Tzu—the Merrilee manifest group of survivors—were stuck in the outside dimension of Merrilee and had no idea what to expect. The astounding oddity was that Jacqueline and Kelly Marie were alive, and Aquinas, Hildegard, Che, and Sun Tzu were dead.

The overriding question: was John alive or dead or both? Because Lucifer and John were walking as one. It was like John was speaking in front of a green screen, and Lucifer was flipping 250,000 copies of the crowd.

2

Watching the heads nod are Solomon, Muhammad and Jesus Christ. The two old men of history and the invention of the Devil himself. Even though the gathered group came at Merrilee's command, Solomon and Muhammad were circumspect over the entire affair. There is something about time-in-grade that gives that validity.

Christ was another matter. He was the dissimulation fact-set etched in every human brain for two millennia. Jesus Christ was the Enigma. The marionette of the Devil—the hollow man of history. For some reason, the mix of the group was designed. By whom was the drifty question floating among the members.

The perspective of talent was based on Jacqueline and Kelly Marie. Jacqueline, the 21st century power hitter from Canada who could operate seamlessly in the fifth dimension. Kelly Marie was Lewis Carroll's "Looking Glass."

"There's no use trying," she said. "One can't believe impossible things." And then she pulls it off.

These two women eclipsed the group. Jacqueline and Kelly Marie were *cat riders* continuously operating the six dimensions.

The men were versions of flawed ego—stuck in the agency of psychoanalytic theory. Always in the mirror of *no one could be better*. Hopelessly primitive. Of course, there was talent among men, but the men were like a toolbox kit—inert until at the hand of a woman.

Then there was the bifurcation of the *alive* and *dead*. The magic crossover position that Kelly Marie and Sun Tzu managed to Shanghai into a piece of vintage U.S. Forest Service equipment—the Osborne table. This set of specifications, along with conventional wisdom and magic moments, captured by Merrilee, the daughter of Ra, the Sun God of Egypt.

Kelly Marie continued to hold Merrilee's attention as she, once again, asked for an explanation.

"Wouldn't this be better if you just told us what's going on here?"

3

As Merrilee looked to Kelly, and then the group, she focused on Jesus.

"Jesus of Galilee or Jesus of Nazareth. Which one do you prefer?"

John (Lucifer) interrupts. "Call him 'Christos' as the one I anointed for my mission. That way you cover Hebrew, and we won't piss off King David, who still believes Christ is on the way."

Saint Thomas Aquinas is holding his head.

"Jesus Christ, John! Can we dispense with your usual hyperbole schoolyard bullshit and let Merrilee speak!?"

The relationship between Aquinas and John was the authentic platform among all who knew. It was Aquinas who went to find John in Paris. It was Aquinas who walked with John, not realizing he was walking with Lucifer. Aquinas understood the curiosity of John. Their conversations became written concisely in modern literature. Their arguments over *space and time*. Aquinas's admissions over *time dilations*—how he was unable to discern John's intentions after the fact—giving John a moment of conversational victory over Aquinas.

Their conversations in the Paris Café Society next to Place Saint-Michel became the table talk of la préfecture de Paris (Police).

Everyone in the group was fitted with purpose by Merrilee. The oddity of that was how unfamiliar Merrilee was with the environment outside the fifth dimension. Both Solomon and Muhammad saw the dichotomy in the Merrilee mental structure—on firm footing one moment, and off-balance the next. Her power, however, overrode any attempt to overthrow her position. Even that was odd because her Hyperstrike power was almost a latent defect. She was like a living "Enola Gay" flying around with the Atomic Bomb, code-named "Little Boy" and refusing to open the Bombay doors over Hiroshima.

None of this was lost on the women in the group. They understood the strength of power without execution.

Hildegard of Bingen was beatified by Pope Benedict XVI. She was obviously late to the Saint table, a problem women seem to have in the male gender lockup of the Holy Roman Empire. But, in this group, she was some combination of Gloria Steinem's political activism and Helen Reddy's "I Am Woman."

John spotted her right away as the Second Wave activist of the Seraphim. John's induced capacity as Lucifer gave him a leg up on Aquinas who, although brilliant and a Doctor of the Church, was outsized by the man who had a smack-down with the Archangel. John was only one percent back of God. That way good and evil kept a balance—albeit tentative.

But the selected mix of people tossed a very wide net. Two of the men: Sun Tzu and Che Guevara were all about war—the fight. There was age and experience with Solomon and Muhammad. There was the prettily cunning and insight of Jacqueline. There was the incisive logic of Kelly Marie. All of this on the needle head of power between Merrilee and John. John, as Lucifer, held a decisive edge against Merrilee; however, he was, by trade, an academic. "Faculty Member of the Year," as it were. So, his understanding of science, including quantum mechanics, kept him on the margins of discretion. John also had a cunning way like Jacqueline. A social trickery. What you see is not what you get.

So, it was this particle-package of arguments and religion who were about to learn what Merrilee had in mind. The entire group maintained a keen awareness of strategy. They were effectively here against their will, while knowing that they were saved from utter extinction by a starseed from NGC-234. None of this made sense unless there was a plan.

Lucifer set the tone as he spun John's head toward Merrilee.

"I can hardly wait to gaze upon your irrational rubric of tranquility."

Before Merrilee could speak, Kelly Marie came with *"Wait!"* Instantly, she had everyone's attention.

"It seems to me that we are in a suspended state of existence. We are alive and dead. A collection of Schrödinger's cats, if you will. That means we are in superposition with random circumstance. We are standing in someone's version of the 'Fermi paradox.' What if this is what is? What if the vastness of the Universe is just vast and nothing else?"

Aquinas loudly clears his throat and looks left—at about 10 o'clock on any analog clock.

"Kelly Marie, let me acquaint you with the Five Proofs of God."

5

Aquinas, as "Doctor of the Church," enjoyed a great deal of celebrity among Seraphim. However, his continuing popularity flew in the face of 21st century logic. Aquinas was a solid 13th century thinker. His world spun around action and reaction in the most elementary context. Maybe that's why people liked him—he was simple to understand.

"*Kelly Marie, there are five arguments demonstrating the existence of God. I wrote them in my* Summa Theologica *during the 13th century. I will read them to you.*"

John shouts over the group, "*Holy Shit! Do we need to endure this yet another time?*"

Aquinas looked stunned. Although a rancorous relationship, John and Aquinas seemed to base their interactions on discretion.

"*My dear Lucifer/John, clarity of expression has never been your problem. You lost your fight with God. He was your contemporary—he still is—but you tore the paper. You ripped the relationship beyond repair. God never wanted that. It was your emeritus grab for power—your mind-blowing ego—that condemned you to the fight of fights.*

"*Think about this, John, what if you had won the fight. What if the Almighty Power now rested in you? You care about nothing. The Universe would be consumed with fear. No hope. No direction. All of space-time would be in tatters.*"

John's neck ripples as he raises his right arm toward Aquinas. Hildegard lets out a shuttering scream. Aquinas breathes back in fear, then silence. Nothing happened. There was no Hyperstrike.

Merrilee lingers a smile like Bastet, the terrifying cat she could be. Jacqueline looks at Aquinas. Then speaks.

"Aquinas, why don't you read the Five Proofs of God to Kelly Marie."

As Aquinas begins to read, the paradigm changes. Kelly Marie has become her own case of diagnostics.

"All of you——ALL OF YOU—are a case of *laissez-faire* intellectualism. Full of your own puffery. It was Sun Tzu and I who saved your sorry asses from extinction. It is my Euclidian geometry that moves you from space to place and back again. Maybe you will remember that if I hadn't managed to get you off the last train to Birkenau, you would be a pile of ash in a concentration camp."

Jacqueline turned to John. "She's right, you know. You were there. You were there in your masquerade. You would have let us die if it hadn't been for Kelly Marie. I was new then. The adventure was on the horizon. Everything was exciting and then, in one of your caustic moments, you put us on the train to Birkenau. To a hot hell of death in a brick gas chamber. You, John, are the personification of Evil!"

John gives her the Devil's determinism: *"Well, Jacqueline, in your paradigm of intellectual systems, you finally got it right."*

Jacqueline and Kelly Marie were remarkably clear of mental slag. Hildegard of Bingen stood alone as the poet and scholar. It made developmental sense that the women outsized the men and were, yet, marginalized.

It was John's genius of Evil that disturbed Solomon, Sun Tzu and Muhammad. However, under the gaze of Lucifer, Sun Tzu found his own mark in Nara, Japan c. AD 760, and he was popular across cultures. The great generals of history from Oda Nobunaga to Tōgō Heihachirō followed his teachings as tactics. He was the daily wear of the daimyos and shōguns.

Solomon was the gender cannon of these three. Women claimed him for his intuition. He was the observer. He was thought wiser than the sages of his reach in Egypt and the Middle East. His love poems in the "Song of Solomon" became so popular that scholars moved them away from religious implications lest his apocryphal wisdom dominate all of humanity.

Muhammad understood and capitalized on the value of the one-on-one encounter. Unlike Sun Tzu and Solomon, Muhammad put his plank on direct talks with God. It was God who commanded Muhammad to teach the people. Muhammad was the master of the miraculous journey—his stop-off to pray with Abraham, Moses, Jesus, and others on his way to Heaven wasn't questioned.

John understood these men. John studied their methods; their understandings. John was the observer with the Devil's tail. It was John who understood there was no omnipresence among mortals, or deities. John was the Master of Physics—of time dilation—of the warp of time.

Now, in the presence of space-time, Merrilee's state of being managed to expose the mettle of the men. In this, she opened the door to the women; for them to see the men as they were, not as they might be.

Aquinas and Che Guevara were flummoxed by their own revelations. As they were opened to the women, they were seen as born generalizers of political fanaticism. Both could ricochet from point to point to make their moment.

The male group mix was a frightening study of the flaws of evolution—not Creation. The anomaly among men was Jesus Christ. He was the invention of John as Lucifer. Lucifer was the unchallenged master of the power grab. John managed to distort the mind of man with Jesus Christ as a false flag. An idea to be followed like crumbs of bread to the snare.

All of this set the tone for a Machiavellian mix of gender war.

7

Merrilee moves to the front of the group—still in suspension but with animation. They were free to exchange barbs, however not free to escape. Merrilee waited until she had everyone's attention. Then she said, "We will be using the Fibonacci number to move this forward."

The group was stone quiet. To admit being unaware of the Fibonacci number was not good form. Aquinas was first to speak: "*I used Fibonacci in my Five Proofs of God.*"

Hildegard retorted: "How does that work, Aquinas? I get it that Leonardo Fibonacci was a 13th-century mathematician, but the sequence was not defined until Munsey 1914 AD?"

Aquinas became the manifestation of Munsey's Weekly. *"For me to know and you to find out, Hildegard."*

Hildegard did not smile. They weren't in New York, and this wasn't Munsey's magazine, so what was Merrilee's point? What was she saying, as Kelly Marie came with her second rejoinder, "WHAT Merrilee! Just What the Fuck—WHAT Merrilee?!"

There was the expected discontinuity of the moment.

Then, Merrilee began.

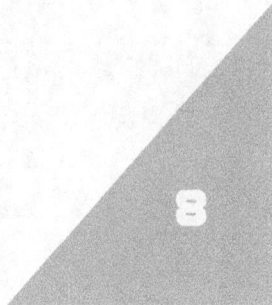

Merrilee was positioning herself as the archetype of dominion.

As she begins, she addresses Hildegard of Bingen: "I am here for a variety of reasons. However, Hildegard, you are my prime mover. It was you whose frequency began to shudder the cosmos. Your distain for male domination. Your unwillingness to be marginalized."

Hildegard's image flashes curiosity as she cocks her head to one side. Solomon picks up her curiosity.

"I find it refreshing that it is women controlling our circumstance."

John moves the tone quickly into the 21st century with "Yeah, right!"

Merrilee turns to John . "You, Lucifer, become the manifestation of whether God's existence can be established by reason alone. There are influential arguments that you may be God. That there never has been a true God of gods. That you operate as the Devil and God in some quantum state of dark matter. That you trigger religious experience and revelation as the yin yang of good and evil."

John smirks. "So, thee Merrilee, are you arguing a priori or a posteriori? Are you trying to convey the idea that God and the Devil are simply one's experience? Are Good and Evil nothing but brain chemistry? That revelation and tree fairies are weighed the same?"

"*How Shakespearean, John!*" comes from Aquinas. "*God is the prime mover. It is the primacy of action and reaction that becomes the proof of God. The argument that 'First Cause' could be the Devil finds no source in time. God is the first and final antecedent.*"

"Nice try, Aquinas," comes from John.

Jacqueline's brain is fighting to maintain measure.

"What the hell are we doing here!? Is this some kind of goddamn theology class? We are in who knows where with a cat lady who has Thor as a buddy, who eats snakes, who controls us with dramatic pause, and apologizes for not knowing who she is in a time dilation. Do any of you have an actual question—or are you happy to be a sack of philosophic ponderables?"

John reaches toward Jacqueline.

"Don't touch me, you asshole!"

Kelly begins to laugh. Then everyone—even John—starts laughing.

Merrilee slowly raises her hands, then her eyes. She is instantly of something else. She is origami change in real time. The light changes around her. There is transparency. She seems to fold and unfold. Blinding white light radiates around her. Her arms and hands extend to touch . . . and the manifestation begins.

Merrilee ignites the hexadecimal 0080FF between her arms. Then at 220 degrees of hue between blue and cyan in Blue White Azure—settling into her hands—the Scorpion.

9

Conversation among the group stopped dead. The reality of being simultaneously alive and dead was always on the table in the outside dimensions, but Merrilee was holding a Zodiac consolation in her hands. She was holding the protector of John and the antagonist to Mars, the God of War. The Scorpion.

The senior players like Solomon and Muhammad seemed to see a foreboding signal in Merrilee's reach into the outside dimensions—this 'show-and-tell' demonstration laced with unimaginable capacity. Che Guevara, accustomed to war, began to postulate what this show of strength might mean.

"Merrilee, una demostración espectacular!"

She stared at him—a blank expression. She looked away. She lowered Scorpius to her belt line—about at her waist. Then she looked down. She examined Scorpius like an eagle watching a rabbit. Her eyes had nictitating membranes blinking—like moments before a kill.

It was the most intimidating thing Che had ever seen. This snake-killer woman—maybe creature, maybe God—was blinking like an eagle before dinner. Che looked away—down, to his left—like a cowering animal. Out of character but real. Merrilee's bearing had reduced the seasoned jungle fighter to a quivering dilettante.

All the rest took the call deep in their being. They were truly in the presence of a deity. One who could masquerade as a woman, a cat, or an eagle—but steal from mythology to be anything she wanted.

Hildegard, Jacqueline and Kelly Marie were less taken with the whole affair. They watched as Che collected himself away from his own

Samson Agonistes drama. These three were symbolically on the other side of Merrilee's membrane. The semipermeable cosmic screen that allows gender to leak through. Fundamentally, Merrilee was a woman, and so were they.

10

Jacqueline turns to Kelly Marie: "I think we are about to get locked into a series of ephemeral power demonstrations by a starseed who is still trying to figure how to hit her ass with both hands."

Aquinas coughs—then laughs.

Merrilee lowers the Scorpion to her feet and Scorpius begins to grow. Trochanters clattering with the stress—gangs of eyes tracking in random patterns—but still very composed. Jesus stacking clay dishes with bread and fish was good but, this was eye-opening. The Scorpion gives a dramatic pause and turns his lateral eyes to Merrilee. "Thank you."

Sun Tzu smiles at Kelly Marie with "*Our magic Osborne has some real competition, I would say.*"

Kelly Marie agrees with reservation.

"Sun Tzu, what you and I accomplished will never be matched. We became the 'Beam me up, Scotty' manifestation of the multiverse. We were the first. It's up for grabs whether the Israelites captured Jericho, but you and I captured space and time."

"*Wow, Kelly. Just wow! There are times like this when you are so on top of your game.*"

Kelly Marie smiled back at Sun Tzu—did a symbolic pickup of a flat rock, and with same, skipped it across an imaginary pond. These two knew who they were. But even better was the mix. Sun Tzu dead—Kelly Marie alive.

Merrilee was a work in progress, a retrospective trying to match her past with her capacity. The women were now together, including Merrilee, within arm's length of each. Hildegard opened:

"Merrilee, do you know what you just did? Do you understand what a strife-filled environment you can create? Do you understand the enduring agonies of witness to your power?"

And it was the Scorpion who answered, "No, she doesn't."

11

The Scorpion begins speaking through the Code of Hammurabi. *"Merrilee is unique in her manifestation of legal tradition. She is like the stone stele of Marduk at Babylon. She is sent because of dialogues with the Pharisees."*

Everyone is frozen in a kind of overwhelming wonder. The casuistic law business coming from the Scorpion is completely unexpected. Solomon and Muhammad are quick to recognize these bodies of the Old Testament.

"We indeed have the 'cosmic impulse' among us," comes from Muhammad.

Solomon agrees with a nod to Muhammad.

Che, Kelly Marie and Jacqueline are the current century players and only occasionally dip into the Old Testament. So, the 'Code of Hammurabi' stuff is bewildering.

"Are you getting any of this, Jacqueline?" comes from Kelly Marie.

"No."

But it was Che Guevara who set the frame. "Look at the Scorpion!"

Scorpius was shimmering and losing structure. He was changing into binary particles. The Scorpion, obviously, came to them in 'Superposition' . . . but from what?

Now the environment was getting scary. Too many events from outside dimensions. Merrilee was in some kind of flow with fundamental atomic structure. The Scorpion was all but gone. Just a fuzzy buzz of particle noise.

Merrilee was as bewildered as the rest. She was in the 'flow' and didn't know why. And the answer was disappearing into cosmic dust at her feet.

Hildegard of Bingen looks to Solomon and Muhammad. Their collective six eyes are instantly in unison and, Hildegard says "Merrilee is the 'Origin of Law'."

12

"You know what we have here, Kelly. We have the manifestation of Alvin Toffler and 'Future Shock.'"

Jacqueline was never without a position. She was strategic to the core. She could feel the effect of information overload distorting Merrilee's bearing. Jacqueline could sense Merrilee was struggling to know who she was while trying to maintain some form of psychological equilibrium. But it was Jacqueline's abrupt command posture that kept her out of Merrilee's trust. Jacqueline was an expert shot caller; however, it was Kelly Marie who had the confidence of Merrilee.

"Well, if it's Toffler we have, Jacqueline, what's the fix?" slides in from John.

"So, John, no surprise that you are in our conversation."

"You're quick, Jacqueline, but now you are talking to *me*, and I have only two opinions: Perfect and More Perfect."

Jacqueline snarls at John. "You are such an anal pore."

"Is that your watered-down version of 'asshole,' Jacqueline?"

He keeps pushing. "Merrilee is in a shattering disorientation. While the Scorpion is declaring her magisterium, she produces random hat tricks. She's got no focus.

"She is like a Joker stuck in the wrong deck—a commander with no army. She can keep all of you entertained with her power tricks but when it comes to targets downrange, she can't take the shot. Merrilee is stuck in a dichotomy of good and evil."

"What about the rule of law the Scorpion recited, John?"

"That works if Merrilee can make the distinction between scoundrels and angels, and I am not seeing that capacity. At least, not so far."

"Well, she got us all here, John. That's more than you could do!"

As the group listened to the dialogue, it was Hildegard, the writer and poet, who distilled her own observation: "John and Jacqueline are becoming the "Swan Song" and "The Bear" in a Chekhov translation.

13

None of this is lost on Merrilee. Her exercise of discretion has become wearing. She needs help. Kelly was trying to explain to Aquinas the structure of the problem. She was using terms he didn't understand.

"You see, Aquinas, it's like we have an autistic kid at recess. She plays hoops and volleyball with her classmates, then when the bell rings, she walks to the fence, squints her eyes, and blows up a car. Then she laughs at how high the flames are rising into the air."

Aquinas utters, *"I think I'm understanding."*

"Okay, Aquinas. How about this. 'She puts fire upon the Basilica across the Roman stone throughway. The fire reduces the Basilica to ash and smoke.'"

"By God's bones!!" comes from Aquinas.

Muhammad turns to Solomon. *"I think he understands."*

Che Guevara can't help himself and jumps in.

"I was Comandante "Tato" in the Belgian Congo. I taught French to the Cuban fighters. I wrote the manual of guerrilla warfare, *La Guerra de Guerrillas*. My picture is on Bank Notes BANCO NACIONAL DE CUBA.

"I suffered propaganda. Was so hungry I had to eat my mule in the jungle of Bolivia. I know she is scared. I know she is powerful. I know she fights for a cause. Haydee Tamara Bunke taught me. I will teach Merrilee."

"Haydee Tamara Bunke!" comes from John by force of passport. "She was a fucking German deep cover agent! She was 'Tania' in your bed. You didn't know shit, Che! She was a spy in your own goddamn camp."

"I turned her, John. You know I did!"

"Che, Merrilee is not a German hooker swatting mosquitoes in Bolivia."

Both Che and John begin to smile—then laugh.

"Ok, Che, you got the ball. I know you know your shit. Teach this starseed from NGC-234 how to focus on her mission. Not to worry that she has the power of 25,000 suns. That she can turn you to vapor with an eyelash and can bring the Scorpion back from the dead . . . . No problem, Che. Go for it."

Jacqueline, Kelly Marie and Hildegard of Bingen all walked toward Merrilee in unison. Jacqueline opened with, *"Not so Fucking Fast, Boys!"*

14

Jacqueline starts to press: "Heterogeneous packs do not tip over quite so easily, John. Or do we need to give you a demonstration?"

The banter conversation between Che and John had just welded the women into a unit. The Devil was a foreigner to this kind of a situation—the emotions of gender—lacing members into a wolfpack. Jacqueline made a risky decision with her implication of solidarity, but she was, after all, a shot caller in the rarefied air of her Vancouver C-Suite. It was instantly clear that Jacqueline had drawn a symbolic line in the sand. Kelly Marie and Hildegard were folded behind the line by association. An automatic truth in culture typically ignored by the self-confidence of the male gender. The men were instantly facing a flying wedge of women—one with the power to kill everyone with the flick of her wrist.

The "Boys," as Jacqueline referenced, were in disarray in this moment of obvious power-based politics. Aquinas, confused. Solomon and Muhammad, flummoxed. Che and John stopped laughing. Then John looked straightaway at Merrilee.

"Your unsophistication in this moment is glaring, Merrilee. You are nothing more than your father's broken dream."

The wallop of fear shot through both sides of the line. John had just put everyone at risk. Merrilee could sense what happened. She was in a peloton of sympathetic cohorts. The women were shoulder-to-shoulder with her. Hildegard moved her time-in-grade experience to the front.

"You do not need to meet his challenge, Merrilee."

John, now forming up as Lucifer, snickered, "Nice call, Hildegard. Is your champion starseed in the wrong weight class?"

"If you start making this about retaliation, John, nobody wins." Sun Tzu is obviously fed up with the theatrics. *"I wrote the book, and you seem to be forgetting how we got here. Merrilee neutralized all of us—including you—under the fire of Mars."*

John snaps, "Wrote the book! You wrote the fucking book, did you? I am the one who fights the Archangel, Sun Tzu! I am the snake. You are the mouse."

"And I am the one who neutralizes you, Mr. Snake, with my rubber suction cup."

With a light laughter smile, Kelly Marie raises her arms to address the shoulders of the women. She pulls them in with . . . "We are watching the operational talent of the dominant gender, ladies. What do ya think?"

15

John was trained well. His existence approximated an exoplanet of the Devil. John revolved around the mass of Lucifer—becoming a reinfestation of Evil. Everyone was familiar with the ways of the Devil—but not effectively.

Lucifer was John, and John was Lucifer. The Machiavellian plan to overthrow the power of Heaven was afoot. The paradigm of John and Lucifer was the shift away from light. The mix of this group was existential.

Merrilee was the energy budget of light. She was the perfect horizon of spiritual geometry—the rotation velocity of good over evil. But, she was new to that position and Jacqueline was the first to notice. The first to notice that without a steady hand, Merrilee could generate amped-up cosmic inflation. Jacqueline could feel Merrilee's power to be random quantum fluctuation. She could see Merrilee flashing as the giver of life in the order of time.

Aquinas was stuck on "God" as the giver of life. When Merrilee blurted out some form of "Hat Trick" magic, Aquinas saw First Cause. He saw God perspicuous as man in the moment.

The remaining members of the group were circumspect. Time-in-grade caused them to remain in stride with creationists' understanding. Merrilee was a tool—but whose tool?

It was Sun Tzu who was envisioning a hypothetical rubric around Merrilee. It was Kelly Marie who saw the geometry of a plan going forward. It was Che Guevara who saw the positioning as War Craft.

As was typical of their association, Solomon and Muhammad felt everything came in its time. They saw Merrilee as the manifestation of history. A kind of 'here we go again' mentality based on their cross-culture relationship involving the Canaanites, Philistines, Assyrians, Babylonians, Persians and, finally, Alexander the Great. Could Merrilee be the second round of Hellenization? Could she be the daughter of Alexander instead of Ra?

Yes. This was personal to everyone. The ultimate quest for the alloy wheel of time.

Che Guevara was uneasy. Wanted to move.

"What's next?" he asked. "How do we get away from this gray matter we're in? It's uncomfortable," he said, following that with, "I don't like it!"

Merrilee made a kind of clearing-away sign—like clearing a table with the sweep of her arm. The space in front of her went black. Sort of made a humming sound. As space came into focus, there was lots of light as background. Merrilee looked at the group and said, "This is a 'time transit.'" She stuck her head into the space. Her body began to be pulled. She looked like a passenger sitting next to a blown-out window in an airplane at altitude. She was being sucked out of the hole. Then she was gone.

"FUCK" snorted Jacqueline. "What the hell was that?!"

John began to laugh. "I knew it!" he said. He walked toward the opening. He was gone.

In a bit, Hildegard of Bingen faced the opening. Aquinas hollered, *"Wait, Hildegard!"*

"Wait for what?" And she was gone.

16

There was a scramble measured in split seconds as the remaining group members addressed the opening. They were gone—all were gone.

The space around was with Andromeda, the daughter of Cepheus.

"How did we move from gray matter to the house of the King of Aethiopia?" asks Aquinas.

The environment was as if deeply hidden in the flock wallpaper of existential physics. They were in the royal house of Cepheus, which was the galaxy Andromeda.

Sun Tzu immediately asked if the group was moving as he looked around the house of the King. As she answered Sun Tzu, Merrilee was working her way forward.

"We edge away from the 'time transit' at 299,792,458 meters per second, Sun Tuz."

None of this was making sense, collectively; however, to John, it was making very good sense. Merrilee's time transit had just opened the door to her Quasar absorption lines. John suspected she was tracing backwards as she moved forward but he couldn't establish her scope syntonically. Now he knew her track and could act accordingly.

Kelly Marie and Sun Tzu were unable to constrain the geometry of the Universe inside the house of Cepheus, so they were also playing in the back track absorption lines. The astounding revelation to the senior members of the High Holy Order was that the Universe was functionally an equation describing infrastructure. The entire group was moving at the speed of light through an algorithmic data set. And the daughter of the King of Aethiopia was moving with them.

The freedom of golden orbs and music and cherubs and gauzy overhang of Heaven was hyperbolic bullshit. Something oversaw the whole shitteree. The senior members of the High Holy Order began to cluster in disbelief. For multiple millennia their spirits existed in heliography. None of their perceptions were accurate. This almost haphazard move by Merrilee flew in the face of all they understood to be true.

John was taking it all in stride. Being Lucifer, he was delighted—as John was cunning. As a member of this group, he was his own wolfpack. Then, while basking in his invented glory, he called for the question in rapier wit, "Who among you understand that you exist in an untenable waffle of God's irrationality?"

17

Every personality in the group came into play. John had opened the door to a 'which box' hypothesis. That God, as this group understood, was a quantum enigma.

Kelly Marie did a twist toward Jacqueline, "Are you getting this?"

"To the extent that my brain has been hiding in the closet, I am. But there is a bigger issue. How much of this is Merrilee getting?"

Kelly Marie picked up her thought. "Yeah, like we are on the back side of the setup by Ra when he was angling to be the new god of gods. He is the one who arranged for Merrilee to receive the power of the Quasar in Pisces, but he may not have told her why."

Jacqueline agrees. "That's a point, and when the Mars thing happened around Scorpio—when Lucifer hit her with a Hyperstrike—Ra's original plan fell apart in favor of him saving his daughter."

"Wow, Jacqueline! You and I have precedents for some history."

"Yeah, right."

As Jacqueline agreed with Kelly Marie's sequencing, she came with her own capstone.

"Merrilee is operational with the power to support the takeover of Heaven; to take over everything, and she is holding it like an automaton."

"Yep, I see that. She comes with these 'off the wall' examples of power. Then her expression is like 'What was that?'"

Kelly Marie calls again for the question.

"Well, shit. How do we do an end around with Merrilee, so she gets on the rails? I mean, how do we do that!?"

Suddenly, from what appeared to be from nowhere, John takes Kelly Marie by the arm and spins her to face him.

"You don't do that if you have any fucking brains!"

In an instant, the history of cohesive relationships was destroyed. John was shimmering as Lucifer, and he was the enemy.

18

"Okay, okay" comes out of the pack. "I think we all know who the fuck we are!"

It was Che, and he was about to put it all in his perspective.

"John is the enemy. Merrilee is a gift from somewhere. All the rest of us are complicit in the original conspiracy to find out how and why John was drawing down the frequency of the High Holy Order. I had the same problem. John and I shared that concern. There are those among us who were the inquisitors. The Gaslighters of Heaven. The Holy Ones who were no more holy than prison wardens."

Solomon edges in, *"I resent your tone, Che. You were the bounder who, while hiding behind a contrived revolution, killed people at about the same rate as any day in Auschwitz. You are a dilettante revolutionary with all your brains in your pants."*

Sun Tzu gave a nod to Aquinas. *"Holy Shit, Aquinas, are you going to step in here?"*

"Gentlemen, as the best-known scholar in history I can assure you collectively that your claims are walking on feet of clay."

Aquinas was in the flow.

"All the flaws we have, historically, are pale in the face of why we are having this conversation while sitting in the flocked wallpaper of the house of Cepheus. Has it occurred to anyone that Merrilee just opened the counteractive door to relativity? Are you not curious that around your special loathing she is performing physical and spiritual feats beyond your capacity? Do you not even speculate that we are in the house of a King that is 152,000 light years in size? Maybe you should take your porridge pot and sit on your old

wooden chair; stare out your masonry open-air window and see if you can visualize what's really going on here."

John remained smug in his Devil's power.

Kelly Marie was, as always, profoundly disappointed with the mental vacancy of the collective.

"I don't know why in the hell I bother with you guys. You are a continuous drip of disappointment. If it weren't for me being able to talk with Jacqueline and work with Merrilee, I would be in a straitjacket."

Jesus Christ, who has been quiet for most of the escape from Mars, had a rejoinder.

"Ladies and gentlemen, I am the outlander in your presence. I am the one who, through the cunning of John, managed to keep six billion people under the thumb of the Devil. You are here because you believe in a higher order. You are here because you bought into my story. Now you are here because you are so inadequate you need to be saved from yourselves."

John began to laugh out loud.

"Holy Shit, Christ, you are my kick-ass guy. Nice call. Nobody here is worth our time. We should go back to the Milky Way and see if we can start over with an exoplanet outside the range of some black hole's event horizon."

Merrilee had moved closer to the space around Andromeda, the daughter of Cepheus. In that moment, no one in the group realized what that three-person collective meant by raw power. Everything was becoming intrinsically probabilistic. Cepheus, with Andromeda and Merrilee, was sizing up to be the sway of a control grip dominion. At least that's how John saw it and it turned into a null—total quiet. In an instant the group was bifurcated by power. Good and Evil on display. The Schrödinger equation in high relief. The elementary particles were exciting around Merrilee.

Jacqueline spoke a cappella: "We are where physics encounters consciousness. We are at the command of time. We are at the wonder of the Universe. We are at the Francis Thompson moment wherein . . . 'thou canst not stir a flower without troubling of a star.'" To which Kelly Marie added, "Amen."

Everyone continued in visual high relief. Then, the deafening voice of The House of Cepheus beckoned for accounts: "***Who are thee who walk with me?***"

19

"To the House of Cepheus, I am Hildegard of Bingen, Hildegard von Bingen, Sibyl of the Rhine. I am of noble parents and was educated at the Benedictine cloister of Disibodenberg by Jutta. I am the First Cause of why we walk with your noble house."

Cepheus looked to and upon her. "You, Hildegard von Bingen, are the First Cause of this?"

"I am. I took upon a Raven at the Suzzallo Library to speak with John .To tell him of the question among us. To seek his help in the consolidation of power in the High Holy Order."

"Tell us then, why as Sibyl of the Rhine?"

"To the House of Cepheus, I say unto thee and all who hear this message: When I composed "Symphonia Armonie Celestium Revelationum" ("Symphony of the Harmony of Heavenly Revelations"), I saw Creation as a universal manifestation of man. The medieval church took my work to mean 'men.' A tragic err in concept, art and music.

My work's interpretation became the standing tradition of religious texts. Masculinity became doctrines in codices dominating the evolution of the church. My position to the House of Cepheus is I wrote my work in historical context to be integrated as art—not men. My mission is to change the culture of the Universe to avoid the dominant incantations of men."

Jacqueline leans toward Kelly Marie, "Did you know her position on this?"

"Sort of."

Hearing Jacqueline and Kelly Marie, "What have you to offer woman?" is directed toward Jacqueline from Cepheus.

"You can lower your volume, my dear House of Cepheus. I don't have a hearing problem."

Aquinas lowers his head, side-eyes Hildegard. "She's going to get us tossed into deep space!"

Jacqueline looks to Merrilee, then back to Cepheus as she opens her palm toward Merrilee..

"We are in your House, Cepheus, because of her. That woman is a hyper vector, a black cat at will, the daughter of Ra. I assume you know of Ra?"

"You are to mean the 'Sun God of Egypt'?"

"That's right."

"We know of Ra, and we know of his daughter," comes back from Cepheus.

Cepheus seems to be rising. The House begins to change—like the International Space Station (ISS) might do to reposition. Sun Tzu and Kelly Marie are acutely aware of the change.

Cepheus continues: "The House of Cepheus is the constellation in the northern sky—23 hours right ascension and 70 degrees north in declination. We move to avoid being taken by the monster Cetus. We know that Ra traveled with his daughter Bastet to avoid Apep the snake.

"My daughter Andromeda is to be sacrificed to Cetus," then exclaims, "I am deeply concerned."

Merrilee is still in close with Cepheus and Andromeda. She turns to say, "I share your deep concern. Do you understand the twin paradox of time dilation?"

Jacqueline turns back to Kelly Marie.

"I didn't expect that from Merrilee. I guess I was scared. Maybe I don't trust her. I don't know for certain. But look at her, Kelly. There is something deeply hidden. It doesn't show. She wears it well, but she is in absolute command."

20

Merrilee addresses everyone: "We can save Andromeda from Cetus with time dilation."

"What does she mean—this time dilation?" is muttering among the group. The House of Cepheus is quiet as stone. The group continues to mutter over the order of time.

Merrilee continues, "We know that relative motion is part of 'special relativity'."

Sun Tzu smiles at Che and Aquinas. *"You boys had no idea, did you?"*

"I think we are in the presence of a natural Black Diamond," replies Dr. Che Guevara. "She is pure as white and manages her inclusions as required."

It slips by the group that Che was a doctor as well as a jungle-fighting revolutionary. He goes on, "Merrilee is the cycle of time. We noticed her confusion about travel when she wasn't clear about the timing of events. Now she is. Her *being* has caught up to her *Being*, if I may rely on Heidegger's *Being and Time*."

Jacqueline, now with enough time to see the orthodoxy, defends the Trinity mission.

"We have all been through a great deal. We are in the power of time as well as the moment. We found ourselves in the House of Cepheus. We were frightened of the magnitude , and yet our starseed charge offers Cepheus the path to save his daughter. We are the gift to change the melancholy of existence. Hildegard just gave us the mission statement. We are the riding border clan of the new beginning. We are both fidelity and desire. We are the surety contract of the age, and we have as our contemporary Merrilee, the breast of our horizon hurl forward."

John contentedly rubs under his nose. "Why we don't just line up in a peloton behind Jacqueline and march down the fucking Champs-Élysées."

"You are such an asshole" reminds everyone that Jacqueline's management style can erupt at various levels.

Kelly Marie winks at Solomon and Muhammad, then "I think it's time we ratify the 'save' Merrilee has in mind for Andromeda."

Both men nod to agree.

Kelly Marie turns to Merrilee, "Tell us."

"Time between two observers changes by square root of $\sqrt{(1 - v2/c2)}$." Then Merrilee stands in silence.

"And?" comes from Aquinas.

"We change the notion of simultaneity between Andromeda and Cetus. We will simply move Cetus into another dimension—another universe, if you will. Cetus is gone forever. We will need Kelly Marie to use Euclidian geometry to make the switch."

Merrilee turns to Kelly. "You will move the time stamp so Cetus and Andromeda are using two different clocks."

Kelly Marie wrinkles her nose at Merrilee, who is recovering rapidly from density of the solution. Then Kelly Marie clarifies, "So, we are going to change the order of time—literally?"

"That's right."

The House of Cepheus thunders a declaration: "You have brought my sorrows to an end."

Che whispers to Sun Tzu, "Do you think we can get some mileage out of this?"

"Shut up, Che. Just shut-the-fuck-up!" as Jacqueline reminds Che that gender comes in many formats.

21

"The House of Cepheus is pleased to welcome you to the sanctuary of time."

Kelly Marie is quick to scale the comment, "What, Cepheus, is your dream of the ancient past?"

"The House of Cepheus knows there was Creation to Abraham—there was Abraham to Moses—there was Moses to Saul. We know the reveal of God and Creation."

Aquinas asks, "*Do you know of the book—the Bible that supports Christianity, Judaism, and Islam?*"

Jacqueline, now in full assay of the exchanges, jumps over Aquinas to ask, "What is your time stamp on Creation?"

"*Ego michi non placeo!*" comes from Cepheus.

Andromeda reaches to embrace her father. "You are my father, Cepheus. You are the one who knows. You are the garment of time. Wear it now for these visitors."

"Before you speak, we must set the clock of time between you—Andromeda and Cepheus."

Merrilee places her answer in what Cepheus will understand: "In this moment, Cepheus, we are going to change Andromeda's relationship to the nearest star. You will not notice the change, and that's the secret. Time is a perception based on relative movement. In this action, the clock of Andromeda will go slower in perception of space and time. The clock of Cepheus will go faster. It becomes the manifestation of Zeno's paradox."

"Indeed!" comes from The House of Cepheus. They shall never meet."

"You got it." comes out of Merrilee's mouth. Then she looks confused. Like a cat trying to chew gum.

Kelly Marie scouts the faces of the group, then smiles. "It just happens, guys. We're working on it."

Then Kelly Marie looks to Jacqueline and speaks without vibration, "I can hardly wait for his answer to your Creation time stamp."

Without notice, the Trinity of Jacqueline, Kelly Marie, and Merrilee was unified. Their remarks regarding one another were unbridled, candid.

They became three women calling for the same question while honoring their own collective. In their twinkle of wit, they were inside their own mental compound.

22

Cepheus grasps Andromeda's hand in the clutch between father and daughter.

"There is a precise moment—the time of 'Second Creation,'" he opens to the group. "The House of Cepheus, and others were then. We were told that Second Creation was a 'gateway' to polytheistic culture in spatial time. We did not know what that meant."

Aquinas begins to fiddle with his rosary. *"Second Creation?"*

"Yes. We were told that we were in the 'throes of emergence'; that 'time' was a frangere of the First Creation."

Kelly Marie gives a gentle shake to Jacqueline. "That's 'fractal' in English."

"Why don't we all just sit down," comes in unison from Muhammad and Solomon.

Muhammad picks it up: *"John convinces Jacqueline and Kelly Marie to join in his adventure. However, we are talking about time, are we not?"*

Everyone nods in agreement.

"The third member is Merrilee. We are told she is from NGC-234. Has it occurred to anyone that NGC-234 is within the Andromeda galaxy, also known as M31 or NGC-234?

"Has it occurred to anyone that Merrilee might be standing in The House of Cepheus by design?

"Has it occurred to anyone that Merrilee might truly be from another dimension?

"Has anyone noticed that we are collectively on her *mission—not our own?"*

Aquinas interrupts. *"What about her father Ra, the Sun God? All the history about her protecting the women and children of Egypt? About her and this black cat business?"*

John leans back and laughs, "Well, she does get around."

Jacqueline squints at John. "What are we missing, John?"

John whispers to Jacqueline, "All I know is she is powerful as hell. No pun intended."

Solomon, standing with Muhammad, addresses Cepheus, *"You knew this was afoot, Cepheus. You knew someone would come. Someone to save your daughter Andromeda. You have been waiting long for the change of time."*

Both Solomon and Muhammad understand the abstraction of the moment. Merrilee extends her hand inviting Cepheus to step down. As Cepheus finds his way into the group, Merrilee ascends, turns, and speaks, "I am a Time Lord from the First Creation."

23

"And I am..." John studders. Then he goes on, "If she is a Time Lord from First Creation, I am the dragon who had a hand in her obscurity. God created me only to throw me out. However, she is not of God. No! She is a contrivance of herself—of her preferences of choice. Of her bizarre flutter around love. If she is who she is, I am who I am. She is my target. She is the lurking Nisse of good over evil. I am the dark shadow of her shallow existence."

Merrilee looks down on John. "You are a vacant Shakespearean Junkie."

With that, John extends his right arm into a direct angle toward Merrilee. He sets for a Hyperstrike.

Merrilee smiles. "I disabled your weapon as we escaped Mars. You know that."

"Do you think I allowed that to stay, Merrilee?" John stiffens his arm and rests the other against his torso.

"Wait! Wait! WAIT! just a goddamn minute!" comes from Jacqueline. "Shall we just try and calm down here. Shall we set a moment aside to figure out who is who in the fucking zoo."

She turns to Merrilee. "Why are you here, Merrilee? What about all this ritual Hocus Pocus anyway? Who is this guy Cepheus?"

"And you, John. My fake attraction as a man who becomes Lucifer... WTF, John?"

It was "The taming of the shrew." The scene was Franco Zeffirelli at his best. It was Shakespeare's finest hour. It was Jacqueline flying her corporate flag, snapping it in the face of everyone.

"I feel like we are a tribe of unleavened bread—the gang who couldn't shoot straight.

"I am willing to help you, Merrilee. I am willing to give you all my experience in corporate strategy. I am willing to help you navigate your way to your destination—to your goal. However, in exchange for that, you get to drop all this intangible baggage you sprinkle around like Merrilee's famous fairy dust.

"And, John, if you raise your arm one more time, I'm going to cut it off at the elbow."

Hildegard of Bingen looks to Aquinas. "Well, Aquinas, I guess all is well in the Universe."

Then she calls to Jacqueline, "Do we all get to play?"

Jacqueline sniffs the ozone and says, "Yes."

24

Merrilee is the emerging four-dimensional continuum of time; Jacqueline, the decisive platform with a deep understanding of leadership. Everyone in the group maintains a singular quality of who they are. The exception being John and Lucifer who operate as one.

In polytheism there is a chief god coagulating the ideas of the others. Merrilee is shaping up to be the expostulation—a polytheistic god on the hunt for the chief god. She is triggered by centuries of gender bias with Hildegard of Bingen her marquee example.

Two considerations arise: Merrilee is powerful enough to carry the day and Merrilee is unaccustomed to her station. As a Time Lord, she was operational well before Lucifer invented Christ. That gave her the chops of history; however, in this moment, she is absent the harmony of experience.

Jacqueline makes the carpe diem play with strategic precision. There is a wellness feeling lacing its way through the group. They are not constrained by the cultural draft of Emperors and Pharaohs. Instead, they are about to walk in the shadow of Creation's First Cause masterpiece—Princess Merrilee.

After a nod of acknowledgment, Aquinas brings history into focus. *"If we are at the beginning of a new time, we must be able to comprehend the path forward."*

Cepheus turns to the group. "You have among you Che Guevara, the jungle warrior of Bolivia."

With elbows in play, Che Guevara comes forward.

"That's right," he says, as everyone looks to Che's distinctive sense of self, feeling his words ricochet around. "I will be your lonely candle into the dark."

John snorts and is instantly overwhelmed with tears from laughter. "We are about to be led by history's man of spectacular failure."

"You are not my Camilo Cienfuegos, John! I took out Batista. I will take you."

"Oh, stop it, Che! Jesus Christ, I'm not going to swing at your incapacity."

Jesus is behind Sun Tzu, but his words are to the front: "John, would you stop using my name in your magnified self-importance."

John stiffens his arm.

"I can always toss your sorry ass back to the Greek prison. You have no horizon, my dear Jesus Christ. You are the hitchhiking truant. I am the warden."

25

To everyone's surprise, Christ offers a return. "The root of what you do not have, my dear obfuscated John, is the history of my Hellenic culture. In the fifth century, before you invented me—the Christ—we were already in the 'Age of Kings' and the rise of democracy. I notice you speak from time-to-time about the Peloponnesian War. Well, John, that's plural, my friend. It's the Peloponnesian wars."

John turns to the assembly. "Jesus Christ is as silly as a Heinrich Schliemann discovery. The death mask that wasn't. He is no better than black-figure pottery under the liberation of fine art."

Aquinas looks to Jacqueline. "*Are we now to drag our way through the city-state trash of pretend intelligence?*"

Jacqueline smiles, but John sees this doggerel affront as insolence from his own minion in this theater of inventing the Christ. To her management style, Jacqueline can feel Che Guevara's dwindling candle in the dark and motions to Kelly Marie.

In the foretell of this argument, Kelly Marie, who has a personal relationship with Merrilee, reminds everyone that "In Hellenism, the roots of Greek culture, we are a 'league,' and to that situation we are on a mission to find the Holy Spirit of Monotheism. At least, that's what I believe this is about."

Cepheus looks at Merrilee. Merrilee looks at Jacqueline. Jacqueline looks at Aquinas. Aquinas looks at Hildegard. Hildegard looks at Sun Tzu.

Once again, John starts laughing. "You inquisitors look about as organized as blind mice in King Theseus's maze."

The Merrilee of this moment elevates again and addresses everyone as the powerful city-state they are about to resemble. "Moments ago, Jacqueline offered me her help. I accept her offer—now publicly—to begin this adventure to the heretofore misunderstood High Holy Order."

She directs her hand to John. "As was the Acropolis of Athens, so are we. We will build ourselves on a hill. We will become the fortress overlooking everything. We are not a manifestation of the army of Alexander. We will not carry high towers on our backs to scale the walls. We will be the phalanx that reduces those walls to extinction."

26

Aquinas rattles his rosary as he addresses Merrilee and Jacqueline.

"I understand that my original mission to reposition John was a false flag by Lucifer. It is easy to be cynical now when everything from the collapse of Mars forward has been mysteriously set in quicksilver instead of stone. With that in mind, I believe we, collectively, are ready for the motive behind your actions. I understand the original intent of Hildegard was to reposition gender in Heaven. Are we still on her path, or are we on a deviation while being kept in the dark?"

Aquinas recalls the escape from Mars.

"If it were not for Merrilee and Kelly Marie, we would not exist today. Jacqueline, at the last minute, was saved by the decisive actions of Sun Tzu and Kelly Marie. We all have some 'skin in the game,' if I might use some 21st century vernacular."

"I don't know," comes from Jacqueline. "I just feel that helping Merrilee adjust to her situation is our quickest path out of this—whatever 'this' is—as we go moment to moment. If there has been a chance to escape, I have not seen it."

John, in his fretful play on narcissism, captures their attention. "We are here to find God. The true God. The only God. The God of love and joy and forbearance in time."

Che, who in ways is John's contemporary, is surprised. "I thought you and God were cut from the same cloth. I thought your differences were on method, not power. You, John, are the edge on the other side of the God's sword. As Lucifer, you are the balance of power; as John, you are a dagger threat to truth. In either case, you are the corruption of humanity. And now we are to listen to your acquiescence to the wonderfulness of God?"

"My power is engaging, opposed to love. God walks around with a smile on his face—always elegant, engaging, and persuasive by appearing safe. God is not safe! God is the manifestation of evil. God is the power-mad gladiator of male dominance. He is a gender icon for men. God is a complete distortion of truth. 'God,' my dear people, is the archetype for the Wizard of Oz."

Solomon interjects: *"Have any of your soothsayers ever seen God? How about you, John? You ever seen God? Why don't you provide us with some more of your brilliant, articulate, impassioned bullshit about God."*

"I fought the Archangel. His rank was the highest next to God."

"Higher than you?"

"Yes. So, back to you, Solomon. You ever fought the Archangel?"

"No."

"So let me get this straight," comes from Che Guevara.

"You, Lucifer aka John, invented Jesus Christ as the son of God—the God whom you have never seen, let alone met. Is that right?"

"Yes."

"You do this to subvert the order of the Universe, to gain more power, to bolster your flag, so you can scout for a rematch with the Archangel."

"Pretty much, yes."

"Are you not embarrassed while admitting this revelation among the group?"

"No."

Che smiles. "I knew it. I fucking knew it! John, you are as hollow as a squirrel-cracked acorn."

Hildegard opens her hands as she eyes John. "How does any of this relate to Merrilee?"

"You tell me, Hildegard. You are the Gloria Steinem in this conversation."

"What does that mean, Che?"

"What that means is we have been sequestered through your mental bias against men so you can lead a movement to change your position—both real and perceived—in Heaven.

"You were cunning enough to spot a starseed whose capacity, at the very least, is significant. You have been riding in the back of this bus all along. More than anyone here, you are the one on the hunt for influence over God.

"You are in the flow of your own amazement. Here we are in the House of Cepheus that we cannot measure. With a family who expected Merrilee—not you—sometime to save the day with Andromeda, and you did not expect any of it. You are as knocked back as we are."

Cepheus motions Merrilee to intervene before this medieval spectrum of revelation jerks everyone back into dark matter. She begins to walk down a stairway that was not there earlier. She seems to walk in whatever environment the moment requires.

"As the daughter of Ra, and as, what you call a starseed, I am anxious to reach close to the center of the power of the Universe. I have been to Olympus. I have been the victim of Lucifer's Hyperstrike. I saved all of you from an angry Mars. I watch you argue. Yes, I am the one who brought you here. Yes, Cepheus was expecting me. Yes, I walk with the gods. Yes, my power dwarfs all of yours combined. Yes, I can kill or vaporize any threat I encounter. But that is not the plan."

27

"We, that is, you, must realize adaptations in deep space and time."

This was the first time Merrilee took command in multiple formats. In the past there was a tentativeness to her exclaims. Not now. It was like someone opened a theater curtain and there was Merrilee—the main event.

Everyone weathercocked to Merrilee, except two. Kelly Marie and Jacqueline. They were positioned like a producer/director clutch in a run for the money. Fingers steepled, butts slid forward in directors' chairs, feet crossed. If this were not deep space, it would be Money Ball on Shark Tank.

Jacqueline leaned into Kelly Marie. "What do you think, Kelly? What would Isaac Asimov say?"

Kelly Marie began laughing. "OMG Jacqueline, you have such insight into the ridiculous. If you were a Major League pitcher, would you pitch across the plate or would you spin and pitch down the third-base line just for the Hell of it?"

"No, no, Kelly. I am serious. We are in deep space. We are where Asimov and Robert Heinlein and Arthur C. Clarke could only dream. But they thought about this a great deal. I have given this no thought at all. Merrilee is about to provide her mission plan, supported by, maybe, no clue what she is doing."

Merrilee begins to speak. Everyone is silent with absolute focus on the next few moments.

"I am on a quest for 'First Cause'—for the deeply hidden origin of the Universe."

Then she sits. She looks at Kelly Marie and Jacqueline, motions with her hand and says, "They will fill you in on the details."

"What the Fuck" comes screaming out of Jacqueline. Then she stands and walks toward Merrilee. She turns and invites Kelly Marie to join her. They both stand together with Jacqueline scanning for their focus and attention. Kelly Marie gets nose to nose with Jacqueline.

"Do not pitch this down the third-base line!"

28

Jacqueline turns to face the group.

"The lack of a single authority has plagued society since the beginning of time. At the Universe launch known as 'Time Zero', Merrilee was the emerging authority developed by 'First Cause.' Merrilee was developed to understand the nature of Creation so she could carry the message of primal existence. She was to be the uniter between what we have come to understand as 'God' and the comingle of men and the physics of angels. With only massless fields of evidence, Merrilee was on her own to find her way in these initial moments.

"There is a constraint on natural freedom that was unexpected in Creation. 'Fear', perhaps. The impact of Creation had other problems as well. Mass was developing an impact on gravity. Movement was not as expected. Merrilee was being drawn into the mass of developing bodies in space-time. She was finding her way; however, with all things on the flux of gravity, the way was deeply hidden.

"Eventually, she stabilized in space-time. She intuitively knew she was the product of 'Time Zero'; however, she was still an observer in deep space. By the time she stabilized, Creation was developing along corridors of remarkable growth. The Sapien Man was unfolding his prefrontal cortex to notice environmental change. Merrilee, being from Creation, already knew the story—the cylinder seal from Mesopotamia was the icon being mapped onto the history of man. Symbolically, gender was identified with a Creation story—Man with Woman, Snake, Woman's ear. This symbolism pointed to the natural process of commingled growth.

"For lack of an identifiable deity, the power of men materialized. The 'God' was somehow appearing to men of social consequence and was making demands. These demands were passed on to the women. It was becoming obvious to observers that these men were establishing a system of control over women. As women questioned the motives, man developed a support system—the Devil. If the women did not obey, they would be subject to what these women understood—hot fire in the den of the Devil.

"I know this seems simplistic considering what we know now, but the swindle was working. And the entire affair became a manifest reality. In the order of natural selection, God and the Devil became etched into the fleshy tablets of the brains of man."

Hearing this story, Aquinas interrupts, "*Jacqueline, I know you believe I have an interest in you beyond my vestments, and that is correct. But what I hear you say is God and Lucifer are an evolving manifest reality from nothing. Am I correct in that assumption?*"

Jacqueline looks bewildered. "Aquinas, what story are you referencing?"

"*What you are telling us right now—moments ago—the 'Time Zero' business.*"

Jacqueline looks at Aquinas. "I haven't started talking yet, Aquinas."

Instantly everyone turns to Merrilee.

Merrilee smiles and winks.

Merrilee stood and walked toward Jacqueline. Kelly Marie positioned herself between the two of them. "What you just did to Jacqueline was unfair, Merrilee"

"My harm is, and was, unintended?" as they are now standing as three.

Jacqueline, with no recall, is flummoxed. Aquinas, as with everyone else, is amazed.

Merrilee looks at Jacqueline. "For me to speak through you, Jacqueline, was an example of my capacity in many realms. It was not intended as insulting or harmful. I fully understand you have extended to me your guidance and strategic intuition. I value you and what you represent to this mission and to all of us as a collective."

Then she faced Kelly Marie, "Going forward, we shall be known as 'Tiffany'. I am referring to Jacqueline, Kelly Marie, and me. We are [a] 'Tiffany.'

"From this moment forward, our mission is in play. I satisfied my obligation to the House of Cepheus."

Aquinas coughs aloud and calls for the obvious: *"What is 'Tiffany' to your mission?"*

"Tiffany is a derivative of several languages in antiquity that mean 'the manifestation of god,' and to that end, we are about to become. Tiffany acknowledges universal origin, including the Anglo-French common use. *Tifinie* in French. And late Latin is *Theophania*. I like it because we are women—all three. And Tiffany is the name given to girls born on the day of the Epiphany.

"There is among us, Jesus Christ, who colloquialized his manifestation to the Gentiles, including his divinity as an 'Epiphany.' He—The Christ—is among us in this moment of space-time, as is John, and Lucifer and all the nomenclature they invented to rearrange the values of an expanding Universe. Agreements were made among men. Those agreements will end because, to use a phrase John will understand, today Jacqueline, Kelly Marie and I are the *Epiphany*."

Aquinas coughs aloud, then sneezes. Then Merrilee torques her body to the assemblage before her.

"So, my friends, you ask, what is the plan? My background in enlargements tells me the Universe is infinite. In terms of our theater, it is about 49 billion light years observable. If 'First Cause' is outside 49 billion light years, we have a problem. Not insurmountable, just a step heretofore. We will be on the quest for our own Principia."

"Principia is developed, not found, Merrilee."

"Thank you, Aquinas."

Merilee picks up the pace.

"Aquinas, if you will, allow me to establish some ideas. To the extent that you correct my meanings and syntax, I will be graciously happy. To the extent you use those corrections to change the Tiffany focus, this quest will begin to falter under its own hypoxia."

She turns to the others.

"Okay, everyone, time is on our side. We are travelers in space-time. We will meet opposing forces. Unknown environments. There will be legacy aspects that come from inspiration outside our universal view. We will examine those. We will invite opinion. If we get stuck in the Kuiper Belt, we will twist our way out. We will not be deterred. For as I go, so go you. Each of you, ad hoc to Tiffany, has been selected for cause. Your value will show on demand. I will see to that in real time. Eventually, we will be sitting with First Cause at Time Zero.

"Our known track covers about 1.5 billion light years at the rate of C 299,792,468 meters per second. For the first time in your existence, you will feel frequency and energy in unison. You will rise. You will be personal witness to Schrödinger's equation. You will be able to say 'I was with Tiffany in the duality paradox.'"

As Merrilee stood down, Kelly Marie looked at Jacqueline. "This is so incredibly wonderful," her voice cracking.

Jacqueline queried her, "Really?"

"Yes, really."

Jacqueline understood the connection between Kelly and Merrilee. She knew the adventure was afoot.

30

The class system was established—Tiffany and the others. Aquinas was scratching his head . . .

"Why does Merrilee need anybody?"

Hildegard was slender—tall with siege—but this was not a city-state . . .

"I feel a strangeness now."

As original formers of the idea, these two were now outside the wire . . . not Tiffany players. And even worse, they were subject to the hubris of abject power, no matter how cosmically sainted. "Absolute power corrupts absolutely."

Che Guevara overheard Aquinas and Hildegard and added his perspective . . . "So, we have a starseed who drops in, we dance around trying to keep her stable without embarrassment, she rejuvenates—gathers us like moths to a flame, saves us from the collapse of Mars—and now she owns us."

"In a flash we are strangers—her minions—foot soldiers in her personal war."

"Do you really believe that Che?" Kelly Marie was enthusiastically the solid player in Merrilee's camp . . . a Tiffany member but with ties to the ordinary. Kelly was brilliant, although wide-eyed. Her intelligence protected her like a corona.

"I smile," says John, his alien eyes flickering.

John was Lucifer in context. He drew on his power. He almost killed Merrilee before the strike of Mars. He would not make the same mistake twice. The split between Tiffany and the rest put John with them—the other. He stood in his own sublime exotic power. He remained the Devil and, in that case, the balance of power.

31

Merrilee glanced briefly at her prototype of people—both dead and alive. Kelly Marie and Jacqueline were in a never-seen position on the multiverse. They were operators in both dimensions. All the others were dead. The good news: Nobody seemed to care.

Merrilee was flickering in her space. The kind of miraculous touch one would expect from an interstellar angel. John's eyes were doing the same, but his flickering was distant, distinctive, and disparate. They were like two battleships from opposing countries coming over the horizon in the dead of night—running lights identical, but mast headlights flashing an urgently different message.

The uneasiness was palpable and began to show in odd ways.

Hildegard of Bingen looked stridently at Aquinas. "If you believe I am obliged to invite you up along my hips to expose my naked body, you estás loco!"

Then Hildegard turned to Solomon and said, "Don't interrupt me when I'm talking."

Solomon said, *"You are not talking."*

Hildegard looked at Aquinas . . . and saw not a flicker of a response.

"Did you hear me, Aquinas?"

"No, did you need something?"

The absurdity of the whole affair caught on instantly. Especially as Aquinas asked Hildegard if she needed something and to that Hildegard broke into laughter. Then she hand-signaled Merrilee to come over.

"Merrilee, your null frequency is lingering. We are talking but we are not talking. What you did to Jacqueline is now involving others. I just snapped at Aquinas, told Solomon to stop interrupting me over a statement I was making—but I was not."

Merrilee took a John Steinbeck stance and said, "It's a dirty business—what we are about to do, Hildegard. I apologize. The exercise of my trickery on Jacqueline was a mistake in kind. I will get with Sun Tzu and get this handled."

And Merrilee walked away like she had another appointment with a correspondent at the *Heaven Herald*. Like she was on a go-to-press deadline or something. The reality of invasion prelude was showing. Playful friends to be hardened. This group is about to leave on a campaign into the manifestation of advanced mathematics. The place where time swerved, light twisted in a desperate reluctance to lose position. A place where conscious minds played outside the body politic. A place where Merrilee understood the barrier of strength that was against the shield of her time-in-grade. Regardless of her might, she was sick with worry.

The deep space around the House of Cepheus let loose a horrifying noise. Lights were now fanning the dark. Heaven was a smear of scattered zeta trails. White and blue. Sometimes red.

Merrilee knew it was Lucifer—the odd dichotomy of her life. She was about to move into the operating field of First Cause. She was shouldering a group . . . one of which was the manifestation of deception, of destruction, of fear.

Lucifer and Merrilee stood like stone, looking at each other.

32

Sun Tzu was concerned over the potential for double binds. Merrilee's mix of power with inexperience could cause internal conflicts. A positive response to one person could be a failed response to another. The coming time represented many suggestions for next moves. Positioning herself as the leader put Merrilee in a tricky situation. No matter what she decided, someone was going to disagree. Anxieties will rise as they move toward the space horizon. Her arena will become an Escher circle with tolerance diminishing as she goes.

As situations appear, so will the pressure of observation. Each person's opinion will be measured against another person—both trying to curry favor from Merrilee. A kind of keep the lion happy with fresh red meat footing. A legendary setup for failed management.

All shaping us as a striking step away from 'The Game,' the bedrock codices on how to avoid this very situation. All the gods of Mount Olympus use Merrilee's Game as the benchmark for proper style and positioning. But now Merrilee's 'Tiffany' must lead, command, force decisions in quick time. Tiffany, the three-women command staff, leading a mix of six men and one woman—sometimes moment-to-moment, and under fire.

Backgrounds will come into play. Che Guevara, the jungle fighter, will have little use for consensus. He may become Merrilee's doppelganger in the group. He will understand command decisions are to be followed, not challenged.

Another double bind may become the irony of focus. The group will be consumed with success over failure. That invites internal relationships away from the eye of leadership. 'Free Rider' relationships wherein acquiescence trumps being decisive. So, Merrilee ends up with flawed input based on fear of failure among the members.

Hildegard of Bingen is an artist. Thomas Aquinas is an academic. Sun Tzu is a tactician. Solomon, a sage as is Muhammad. And this is the group nested in an invasion prelude to find the First Cause of the Universe.

The landscape of deep space could be the worst case of heliocentrism around the unknown. What are the looping motions of electromagnetism? Johannes Kepler positioned the sun. Can Merrilee position First Cause? She is a power hitter in the law of galaxies. Will her power work through the strange of infinity?

These moments of the warning glance around noble controversy. The side-eye signals of trial-and-error. For now, all was in the mix of electrifying charisma. The House of Cepheus—all so large—was to become retrospectively small against the first expedition into the order of time.

33

In the tension of the moment, Jacqueline could see the uneasy inexperience of Merrilee.

"You know, Merrilee, earlier you asked me to sort of shepherd you along. You know, like the guy with the long bent stick and the sheepdog. The guy who sleeps with his flock."

"Yes, I did, but you can dispense with the stick and the dog."

"Well, all dogs are not alike." They both laughed.

"Merrilee, in context, there are some examples of who you might be, or be like. It seems to me you have been let loose in the cosmos with almighty power. You know who you are, but you are not certain *why* you are. You arrived at Cepheus to save Andromeda. You stood on the mantel of your own altar. You declared you were of 'Time Zero'. I get all that. I have been watching you since before Mars, since you saved me from Mars, in fact. But I think that after you declared the Time Zero thing, your essence was screaming at you 'Now What?!'"

Merrilee's hands were buried to the knuckles in her metaverse pack.

"Relax, Merrilee. I'm not here to try and expose you. I'm here to give you a nudge along your path."

"And what path is that, Jacqueline?"

"Well, if I may, you want to be grace, beauty, and timeless elegance. I think where you are is barefaced stuck with Hannibal Barca. Certainly, considered one of the greatest tactical minds of all time by famously marching his elephants from Iberia over the Pyrenees and the Alps into northern Italy."

"How did you know I like elephants?"

"It just fits. Power and strength preferring countenance. There is no argument about approval, here, Merrilee. You are in the 'cat bird' seat. Everyone understands that. But to lead, you must gather yourself to harness your power.

"Think of it this way. On the back of these elephants is, maybe, Joan of Arc. A peasant girl believing she was under divine guidance. The girl who saved France in the battle at Orléans."

"What are you saying?"

"I am saying that you are tailored for your job through time. Someone has put you at the table of Miyamoto Musashi, Genghis Kahn, and Simo Häyhä."

"I'm not a Warrior, Jacqueline."

"I know that. But you were chosen for a reason. Let us just do a little proof of concept here and find out why."

Kelly Marie slides over, shouldering a teardrop Maxpedition sling pack.

"Am I in the ideology room here or are you two actually getting ready?"

The women of Tiffany joined hands, as Merrilee turned to her expedition—

"Okay, Everyone, Listen Up!"

34

As her call found its way across the assembly of sometimes heedless ministry, her tone immediately reflected Jacqueline's interest a few moments before. In that instant, Merrilee became the Armory at the Naval Academy, and all the rest were cadets.

This transition was becoming part of the routine—Merrilee's uneasy confidence breaking into a visceral display of unimaginable power. It was not a display, really. It was a thing, a resurrection of self—maybe.

"We will use, as much as we can, the NGC catalog of star clusters."

Kelly Marie gets a sweep of confidence as she realizes Merrilee selected 13,226 waypoints for the move into the perimeter of time. And with that, she began to rifle through her Maxpedition pack, while muttering, "Merrilee does have her shit together!"

John stood tall. His aggrandizing whirl of experience always gauged from the dark side. "Do you really believe what you just said, Kelly?"

"Of course I do."

Here is a taste . . . "So, you plan to follow this on-again, off-again starseed into the order of time?"

"Better than you, John. You cannot figure out who in the hell you are! No pun intended."

Kelly Marie was naive in John's scope of existence. She was loyal. She was intelligent. She was socially comfortable. None of which found their way to John.

John, to this mix, was the odd one out. Nothing was holding him together. He was the Devil's man in a pack of Seraphim, save two—Jacqueline and Kelly Marie. They were walking both sides of the line between life and death. Sometimes John would wattle them mentally as the 'Crossover Twins.' A twist of cosmological conflicts.

Nothing seemed right to John. He could not understand the mix of people. Why were they chosen as they were? He would need more than he had at hand to subvert this expedition away from the primal meaning of the Universe. For John, failure was a success. He needed a mission collapse to support his hold on the dark side of the High Holy Order.

Everyone seemed to ignore that John had been here before. He was the one who fought the Archangel. He had been the contemporary of God. He was the manifestation of Joseph Steiner's finest hour. The egg-crack reality that God, in whatever form, was not immune to another terrifying, destructive visit by the Devil.

35

"Tinker Tailor Soldier Spy" came sublimely from Kelly Marie. "You are never who we know, John."

Kelly Marie—the intellectual partner—was the walking metaverse among them. She, more than the others, would notice a change in John. None of the others could get their arms around the two faces of his enigma. He was the shapeshifting Lucifer, and she was positioned against his change. She watched John like someone watching the wind-changing sand.

Merrilee was pragmatic. She did not seem to enjoy casual chatter. If nature was habitual, she was a constant. That was the problem in Kelly's scope of Merrilee. Pragmatic decision-maker Merrilee was difficult to redirect as her capacity amped up. Only Kelly Marie, it seemed, had the touch in the moment for the starseed.

So, the fix was in. Each member of Tiffany enjoyed a slice of culture that would overlay the remaining components. Aquinas could remain a scholar. Che Guevara a warrior. Sun Tzu the wizard. Hildegard of Bingen the poet-musician, with Solomon and Muhammad, a collective sage. Jesus Christ the interloper with nowhere to go.

As she stood reconning, Merrilee took on a kind of Churchill style. She leaned slightly forward at the waist, fingers to her lips. The only missing element was the cigar.

36

"The magnitude of our success will only be matched by the immensity of the Devil's defeat."

John was crimson with black eyes flashing.

Merrilee did not struggle with her words as she reversed her body angle and stood plumb. In this moment she was the Tribune of Alexandria—her enumerations beyond corporal. As she continued, Che gave John a cool nod, "Are you ready for this oh, hyper frequency, buddy?"

John invited Che to be amputated away from his primal existence. "¡Que te jodan!"

The situation was tense. From the House of Cepheus the existence integer was on the table. The starseed hunter from far-far-away was about to hurry everyone in a fleeting blaze to nowhere. At stake, everything.

Cepheus and Andromeda were riddled with intensity—thankful—now watching. Everyone was concerned.

"Is this what you want, Hildegard?"

"Yes!"

Aquinas was aghast at her acquiescence. Now standing in the optics of mathematical astronomy, they were but a few 60th parts of a minute toward acceleration beyond the reach of the 'universal constant.' Beyond the speed of light.

. . . T minus—Three . . . Two . . . One . . .

37

In a perfectly coherent voice, Merrilee says, "This whole thing is admittedly tentative, you know."

In the moment they were like mice in the Paris subway system. Tiles flashing by on streaks of titanium. Creatures as holographic images. People everywhere in transparency.

"I have wondered what it would be like inside a Cuisinart," Jacqueline said.

"Fuck!" comes from John. "I am playing along with this exercise in space-time, Merrilee. However!"

"Oh, shut up, John!" streaks out of Kelly. Her voice is like Andrea Mitchell's in *Talking Back*. Distortions were everywhere. Nothing was related to classical physics. "We are close to the coordinates, I think."

"You think!"

No one had been speculating on Merrilee's navigation skills before, but her comments in these opening minutes were revealing.

Sun Tzu said—or asked— *"Merrilee, you travel in deep space. You move in light years between galaxies. A 22 million light year is a common day's travel for you, and now you are not clear on the degrees of freedom around our coordinates?"*

"They are still spooling up, Sun Tzu."

"Spooling up? Where did that come from, Merrilee?"

"The Universe has historical order, Sun Tzu. We are moving and adjusting to our entry."

"Our 37-3 entry?"

"Yes." The Universe is *Universes* in our context. We will be in holographic interpretation for some time. Everything must adjust."

"So where did we come from if not the Universe?"

"Existence has no numerical value. It is a constant. It is, in fact, what I simply heard Jacqueline say—'a Cuisinart.'"

"Is there any precedent for this stuff, Merrilee?"

"Ah, I don't think so. At least not in a group context like we are."

Sun Tzu remained flummoxed as he looked away toward the others. *"Is she describing a multiverse?"* he asks himself in the space around. *'I think so,'* he mutters into the same space.

The group seems stationary to themselves, but the environment is unrecognizably swift around them. Nothing is visually crisp. There was no clarity over the mystery. Nothing was cohesive to their space. The speed, color, shine, and texture were interchangeable. Visually they are nowhere and everywhere in real time.

Sun Tzu turns back to Merrilee, *"Are there any typical patterns?"*

"Yes, there is an arc I am looking for." She closes her eyes.

John started with Jacqueline, "We have this eyes-shut starseed leading us on her 'I think I can' mission into the order of time."

As Jacqueline exhaled to his remark, Merrilee opened one eye.

"Be quiet, John. I don't have enough crayons to explain this to you."

38

It is politically expedient for superpowers to deflect confrontation. Starseed Merrilee had just breached that tradition. She tossed it in the face of the Devil. She insulted his power, but the real bite was insulting his intelligence. This kind of situation has a long shelf life. John can become her worst nightmare. And, if he had not planned that already, he would now.

To this group, John is like a jumping spider in the closet. Switching between Lucifer and John at will. Sometimes, not at will. John is his own worst nightmare. He can hatch psychological death, or he can hide in an environment to terrorize and destroy later. Either way, Merrilee's Shakespearean move against his ego tees up a fight at the top.

Merrilee exercised a great deal of power to harness the group as her contingency in deep space. She caught John in vulnerability as he was dancing with his Machiavellian plan around the exposure of Christ. Now, she must decide how to maintain her position against this highest of high-water antichrists.

In their new Lilliputian frame, nothing was changing. The outsized strain of matter was still the hurricane of back splatter. Spin, plumes of silver that should not be. Fast trains passing close—too close. Noise. Then no noise. Updraft float. Nothing connected. Then drop. No movement. The sound frequency matched the light. High blue and low red. Some among the group could hear up to 40,000Hz. Most could not.

The feel of the sound was in Being with thousands of armatures spinning their energy fields. But they knew force fields were not anymore.

Quantum mechanics had classical mechanics by the neck. More complex. More defining. Closer to infinity. Now it was mass and gravity.

The deafening, frightening noise changed. The frequency lowered. The visuals were getting cleaner. Tiles slowing. Titanium rails taking shape. Some images were being redefined. Some disappearing. The striking difference was the electromagnetic spectrum expanded to them like a time lapse opening flower, Merrilee's hand addressing the petals. A panpsychist moment—the flower moving closer to her on its own.

Merrilee looked at John. John gave a snorted derision.

"Do you know where you are, Oh starseed wonder?"

Merrilee lifted a petal angle, so she could focus.

"Would you like the coordinates, John?"

"Don't try to dazzle me with your quantum weirdness, Merrilee!"

John/Lucifer is momentarily face-to-face with his match.

"Why don't we hear the coordinates?"

"Thank you, Kelly" comes from Solomon, now bringing experience to the circumstance.

Kelly Marie edges toward Merrilee and leans into her shoulder, "Don't assume John's failure of imagination makes him safe, Merrilee."

Merrilee seems far away—somewhere but not there. John asks again for their path.

Merrilee says, "Okay, everyone, there will be no more classical terms as the seeds of this expedition. Going forward we are Quantum. We will operate as electrons in superposition."

"What does that mean, Merrilee?"

"It means she still doesn't know our coordinates."

Hildegard turns to John. "Are we going to have to put up with your incessant shit storm this entire trip?"

"Oh my, Hildegard. How contemporary your vernacular!" as the Devil breaks ranks with John, now two beings as one standing directly in front of Hildegard.

"Hildegard, you remind me of black dust on a polar ice cap. When you step into the light, your supporting environment sublimely disappears."

Having had enough of the banter, Che Guevara brings his jungle fighter self into the conversation. "Merrilee, do you have the coordinates?"

"Yes."

"Do you agree with them?"

"I don't know."

"I think you should. We witnessed the delivery system—the flower moving and opening to your hand. In my head, that is communique from outside dimensions."

"What I received, Che, was a series of graphic vectors. Here, have a look. Watch carefully."

Everyone began craning toward Che and Merrilee. In their shared hands was a moving graphic. Whoever delivered the message gave her a mapped-on image of moving arrows on something soft, leather-like. As she moved her hands, so moved the arrows. It was more a compass than a map. When she looked, it opened. When she turned away, it closed. She was holding a sentient Being made of arrows on what appeared to be fuzzy soft tan. The arrows were dark gray to black. The leather-like stuff was creamy white, tan—like one would expect. It was soft and warm. It was alive with observational awareness.

Che looked off and to Merrilee. "You know what you're holding, right?"

Merrilee squinted at Che. "I just wanted someone else to say it."

Che lifted his head toward Aquinas and company. "It's a petal off the flower."

40

The stunned amazement was evident on everyone's face. Once again, the Universe had stepped up to this starseed.

"What does it say, Che?"

"It's not talking, John."

And, again, John curbs his flash of anger so as not to trigger a premature disunion between members.

"67.4 +/- 0.5 (Km/s) Mpc Kilometers per second / per par second." Merrilee was reading aloud the shocking news.

Kelly Marie spun to Jacqueline. "Oh, my God. Did you hear that, Jacqueline?"

"Well, yeah, but obviously not like you did."

"That is the expansion rate of the Universe in every direction, with anomalies for mass and gravity. We are right in the middle of Einstein's General Relativity."

"And?"

"We are in a race with space, Jacqueline."

"How does one do a race with space, Kelly?"

Kelly was quick—a Sapien mix of 'chaos, creativity, and cosmic consciousness.'

She looks closely at Jacqueline and straightaway . . . she says, "Okay, here is a metaphor. Let's use a football team. As the team runs onto the field snorting and pushing and shoving and so on, someone says, 'Do you all notice the field just doubled in size?' Then the team members stop, look around, and they all do a kind of bolt ejaculation. In unison, they say, *'Holy shit, it just doubled again!'*

"What's happening is the Universe is in a multidirectional expansion based on mass and the mass relationship with gravity. A flower just provided Merrilee with the expansion rate. But from what was just said, there are moving arrows on the petal. So, it's not just about expansion."

"So, what do you think our next moves should be, Kelly?"

Jacqueline's hands crossed pulling down on both her sleeves.

"That's your call, Jacqueline. I'm good at thinking. You are the Quarterback."

"Oh, good Kelly—really good! Where are the towels, water buckets and the Game Day Tiger Tea?"

41

"I like your football metaphor, Kelly, but I think we start playing ball with Aristotle."

This was Jacqueline's world view that made her the leader nominee early on. Also, her sense of self. When first approached about the crossover Heaven and Earth idea, her comment was "Unless we go First Class, I'm not going."

Kelly Marie is her ideal contemporary. There was no early connection, but now they both understand who they are to each other. Kelly Marie is a classic academic thinker, but with cachet—a trait Jacqueline admires. Jacqueline is a woman of success with style. Their way of the Tao operational scope enjoys the depth necessary for counseling their NGC-234 starseed, Merrilee.

The Universe was acknowledging these two as a classic executive branch. The platform in their case was the cyclical component of nature in space, with the way and power quickly becoming the NGC-234 cacophony tiger named Merrilee. This package advancing toward the stellar birth of a new age.

Their biblical cohorts advancing with them adjunct to Tiffany, which Merrilee renamed the team. Overall, this group was competitive with other dense galaxies in the interstellar. This group was not about a forming cloud complex. That was cosmologically too simple. Merrilee and company were "in for a penny, in for a pound." Merrilee had the demonstrated ability to vaporize star clusters.

As witness to her power, some outside dimension was guiding all of them toward Aristotle's Empiricism. "The roots of education are bitter, but the fruit is sweet" was his position, and with Plato having taught Aristotle the Theory of Forms, Jacqueline's comment to Kelly was spot on the money. They would be in a moment-to-moment chase of forms. Representations of the gods—but which gods? And which God to be atop this interstellar flux? Was that to be Merrilee?

It was natural for members of the group to mirror Diogenes the Cynic. They could reject the norms of this adventure. What was showing through was its core intent—to be free of the hubris of gender oppression.

Was it the Dharmacakra showing itself to Merrilee? Was it Laozi—religion, or science? Heraclitus and Western thought, maybe?

The entire group has suffered the Sorcery of time together, save the Scorpion.

Now at the frontier, Merrilee had chosen well. Jacqueline, understanding the emptiness in shallow leadership, was to be Ockham's Razor. Kelly Marie, the balance of a Pythagorean triangle.

What could be better?

42

Merrilee acknowledges Sun Tzu but is stopped by John. "Can we dispense with your innocence, Merrilee?" She weathercocks to John as he continues.

"You are receiving these glimmering gifts from the cosmos. Arrows and numbers, and you opt in with a blank stare—your oh, gee whiz platform theatrics. I know, and you know, this is about scale-action pressure. The kinetic theory of gases, to be more precise."

"Why do you bring this up now, John?"

"Because you are gaslighting your fellows, Merrilee. You are playing this innocent wafer being like you want to be sainted by God or something. This is not Fatima and there is no magic light breaking out of a cloud. You are a top-tier player in the interstellar right out of the standard catalog. You are the NGC-234 starseed who uses Andromeda's flag as you camp in Pisces. You have yet to qualify for a big galaxy. You are strong, which I see as a big *so what* if you're not pre-established with a clear objective."

Merrilee pushes off to change her angle to John.

"Of course, Merrilee. You have perfected the up-angle thing. So, now what? You going to feed us some new magic numbers?"

John is dancing for a fight. And, remarkably, he might not win. For all his rhetoric, he doesn't know the actual "wire" of Merrilee.

She smiles. "There are two ways to solidify pressure. All we care about here is the distance between molecules. So, John, how about you explain to us the random motion theory of molecular collisions. No, wait, I will cover that," she says, and begins.

John is flummoxed but saved from himself. He covers a smile, and she gives him a side eye in humor. Because he knows, and she knows, he had no idea what she was talking about.

43

As Merrilee explained the mix of classical and quantum physics to her gathered travelers, Jacqueline was standing away and looking away. Out of expected character, however, Kelly Marie and Sun Tzu were, in unison, watching her.

Jacqueline stood with her arms stretched forward—shoulder high. A slight bend at the knee. Sun Tzu cocked sideways toward Kelly.

"*I think she is holding a 'naginata'*" he whispered.

"Why are you whispering?"

"*Let's just stand still right here and keep watching*" he whispered back. "*From what I see, she is readying herself for a daimyo Takeda Shingen.*"

Kelly's pupils jumped in diameter to almost total black in her eye sockets.

"You're serious!?" she exclaimed.

"*Yes*"

"Oh, my God, Jacqueline and I were just with Minamoto no Yoshitsune."

"*Why!?*" Now Sun Tzu was beyond surprised. "*Why would she send you off to the Samurai?*"

"I would say she is taking some daughter cues from Ra. He gave her up to this legacy moment, but you will recall, when Lucifer hit her with a Hyperstrike, Ra appeared over her like nature's trunk. Nobody gets near if Ra is in the frame."

Sun Tzu looks closely. "*Then, what you are saying, Kelly, is Merrilee is readying you, maybe all of us, for a major battle.*"

"Yep."

"So, what you're surmising here, Kelly, is that our starseed leader is as much a Caste Warrior as she is an Angel?"

"Yep."

Sun Tzu slaps his hand to his forehead. *"Oh, my God, Kelly. Oh, my God!*

And you think Jacqueline knows this and hasn't been speaking to it?"

"Yep."

"Oh, my God, Kelly."

"Umm,, yep. How many gods do you have in reserve, Sun Tzu?"

He gives Kelly a lingua franca hand wave. They both laugh.

44

"For example, we are aware of a hypervelocity star with measured speed of 1.3 million miles per hour, and that ratifies the sample we used..." Merrilee continues to explain the metrics of the mission.

"Is there a reason why we do not use a vessel or craft for travel, Merrilee?"

Che Guevara can be clandestine or imperial. His curiosity typically has him leaning toward traditional examples.

"The issue we have with that, Che, is diversity of reaction speed. As we stand, we are like starlings in flight. We do not see the graphics, but at a distance we are a match for a flock of little dark birds flying along the horizon. Tight in flight and unison. We are a pattern flock. We change the patterns for protection. That change is going on as I speak. For example, right now, you see one to the other as expected in a social pattern. The actuality is you are switching positions—swerving, diving, and climbing, all while maintaining a position in the vortex of a hyper star. As I speak, we are binary free riders behind PSR J0610-2100."

Jacqueline, taking this as a cue, relaxes her stance, lowers her arms, puts down her sharp as a razor naginata, and interjects into the questions and answers around Merrilee.

"So, that puts you in a superposition with yourself."

Both Merrilee and Jacqueline meet this space-time moment like command staff coming out of a bunker on Ie Shima, off Okinawa. The character of this ignition in time could not be overstated. Everyone was stunned at their cohesive swerve in space-time. Merrilee stepped to the side as Jacqueline continued.

"As you know from our history, Merrilee's and my relationship began around the Osborne table when she stuck her teeth in my arm and sent me to the hospital in Helena. In my mind, she still is a large black cat." A smile fell on the group.

"Tension between us followed for obvious reasons. However, that situation changed as we mitigated our fear. Today—I suppose there is a 'today' in some fashion around here—we are working contemporaries. I do not have her astounding swag of power. We all know that. However, we go forward as a team. In the near term, I will carry the deck."

Sun Tzu blinks. *"What's a 'deck', Kelly?"*

"All the cards."

Not everyone was pleased with this announcement.

"If I may, Jacqueline, why do you wait until now to tell us?"

Hildegard spoke as the originator of the idea. The venom was in her to prevail and now she was upstaged by Jacqueline.

It fell upon Merrilee to answer: "Hildegard, you are responsible for all of this—at least in spirit. And you can be proud you have such a collection of cohorts next to you. You are the founder of the mission. But, like any successful campaign into the unknown, the celebrity artist/writer is not on the point."

"Not on the point? Have you looked, Sun Tzu? Is Jacqueline wearing jump boots?"

Kelly's humor was fine with it all. Her intellectual scope was asleep as the rest wrestled with Jacqueline as the lead. Jacqueline looks down at her feet, laughs and continues,

"Hildegard, and everyone, lets us remove 'lead' from our vernacular. Each of us has a selected talent. We were originally carved out for our skill. My skill is tactical leadership to gain traction in adversity. That is precisely where we are in this moment. As we move, each of you will be a 'lead' in the way of your profile. In another context, all of us are flying in unison around the coded leather briefcase we call Merrilee. Our job is to deliver Merrilee to First Cause . . ."

They were surrounded momentarily by a visible low frequency sine wave.

"What are all these strings and humming?" is muttered throughout the group.

"That's coming from PSR J0610-2100. We are the Starling Peloton drifting behind that hyper star."

"Hmm..."

"Jacqueline, would you like to tell us about your samurai sword and Merrilee as a 12th century Caste Warrior?"

Kelly always has a way of changing the story line.

45

There was a long sigh from Jacqueline. Kelly Marie had a quick follow-on.

"You will remember, Jacqueline, it was me who spun Merrilee around as we left the fiery crashing, fragmenting, Mars. It was my decision that saved you from becoming greasy ooze among the common elements."

Jacqueline stood in stunned amazement over Kelly's remark. Then, to her management style, she apologized.

"I am sorry, Kelly—and embarrassed. Here is how we decided . . .

"Caste represents ranked, hereditary among social groups. We are a caste. Merrilee is the Brahma (Teacher). The rest of us are Kshatriyas (Warriors and Rulers). I know this is South Asia 16th century stuff, but it seemed to fit. The other part was discipline. The social order of Samurai represented discipline, and when Merrilee's hands touched the miraculous Sun Goddess sword, *Kusanagi* , we were 'chockfast' solid."

That got a laugh, as Jacqueline did a dancing pirouette with her blade.

"I follow a different cultural tradition," Sun Tzu said wryly, *"but they are correct. It will be we in the discipline of the Samurai whose stoicism carries us to the First Cause. It was a very good decision."*

"Well, okay, everyone onboard?" Che Guevara hiding his smile as he stood in the light of the moment.

"You are such a poser."

. . . Kelly Marie changes the narrative again.

46

As time warped around the talking, it was everywhere. Kelly Marie was edgy—more than in the past. The new information was alarming in that it came after the fact. This was to be a cohesive group after all.

Che remained absorbed in himself. That made him a straightforward study for Solomon and Muhammad. Aquinas was sticking with Hildegard from where it all began. He was less than impressed with the Samurai idea. As a monotheist, the self wasn't as important as the god.

What some misunderstood were the iconic values of symbolism. Altars, flags, decorated command. The Coat of Arms. The tunic over armor—and the blade.

Jacqueline understood she was to be a leader among women and men. And the markers were different. Men would fight under a flag, regardless. Women, only for a valid cause.

It must be a warrior class that challenged the political authority of Heaven. Heaven had become a class of Feudalism. This was to be power against power. Jacqueline and Kelly Marie would bring their segmented Shoguns to the threshold of opposing authority. It wasn't lost on Muhammad and Solomon that these titular rulers were shielding the impact of Merrilee. And Merrilee seemed satisfied to let the glory land at will. All this 12th century Kamakura managing to wrap itself around the sway of starlings ghosting a hyper star.

Jacqueline turned to Kelly. "Tell Merrilee it's time."

From Jacqueline's perspective, their arrangements were finished. Time to step into the signals. They had been in vector space for a while.

No more delays. Merrilee had the set of scalars reduced to arithmetic associativity. Now it was up to Kelly to make some sense of the vector space in linear algebra.

John, now standing with the rest of the group, was swallowing hard against his spider web of emotions. He was having a problem hearing the conversation between Merrilee, Jacqueline and Kelly Marie.

"Do we all get to play here, ladies, or are the rest of us just traction slag on your outer layer?"

"Our linear combination is—av + bw + ... + cz. We will use these in combination with y-directions as we go."

"Do you think Merrilee knows what she's talking about?" dribbles out of Aquinas.

"You fucken a . . . she does!" Kelly lowers her head toward Aquinas as if she were the bull in the Mexico City Plaza de Toros.

47

Kelly Marie did not 'suffer fools lightly.' She was understated in demeanor; however, just below that surface was high temperature physics. Her concern being their existence in the face of nonmolecular systems. The frontier before them, in her thinking, could be a transcendental mazama generating images to be taken for granted while being a path to chaotic flux. A situation impossible to navigate. There was no reason to trust the goodness of the 'First Cause.' They might be approaching a hierarchy of archangels acting as palace guards. 'Tricky business,' she surmised.

To restore order to the Hyperinflation of the Universe, time travel was essential. Somehow, they must get behind the *cause* of *cause*. Change the progressive development of the Sapien advance. To be casual about the creativity and imagination of the Universe was a mistake in the mind's eye of Kelly Marie.

Jacqueline had to somehow manage the entire range of emotions. A gaggle of Saints and sinners traveling with an enigma of women having the power to blow up the Universe. It was a task worthy of a high wizard.

Aquinas was becoming the emergent apologist for everyone. He was completely Socratic. Only questions—never answers. Which is how he managed to get Kelly Marie in the chocks for a fight. She saw him becoming a courtyard freeloader. *Stupid questions from lazy intelligence,* she thought.

"Leaving Star Perimeter now" crackles from nowhere.

Che's head was on a swivel. "Where did that come from?"

"That's Newton." Merrilee left her position, moving to the perimeter, as she introduced the hyperdimensional, 'Newton.'

"There are some notions of deep space we do not understand. Our very own Newton is one of them. 'Black Holes' another. The first black hole man discovered was Cygnus X-1 in 1964. From then forward they became portals for science writers who wanted to send us into another Universe—several universes in fact. Ordinary people routinely try to get their heads around attraction so powerful. It makes everything, including light and time, disappear."

This matter-of-fact science dialogue seemed out of character for Merrilee. There were side-eyes all around.

She went on . . .

"Our Newton came to me by the hand of Jacqueline. I still don't know if either one of them knew what was happening. The Artificial Intelligence (AI) voice from Newton through Jacqueline was speaking of Lorentz transformations in light cones. It was Kelly who researched the cones in these transformations."

Merrilee acknowledged Kelly Marie to speak. Kelly stepped into the conversation like the network news analyst on election night. Up came two light cones tips to each other with a light flashing at the common point. "Here, my friends, is the Lorentz transformation diagram."

Newton's voice comes in over Kelly. "Our navigation strategy is to avoid the singularity around black holes."

Kelly looked around then said, "Of course."

It was like Newton has a trigger mechanism to speak before an answer. Like the "Free Will" argument ongoing between John and Merrilee.

John believes the cosmos makes the decision and tells the brain. Merrilee believes the brain makes the decision and acts accordingly with the body. It makes trivial difference if research advances the answer. Archangel Lucifer and the starseed have their positions and that is that.

Kelly Marie continued, quoting directly from research:

"As we know, astronomers saw the first signs of a black hole in 1964 when a sounding rocket detected celestial sources of X-rays. However, the concept of black holes was hinted at as early as the 1780s and predicted by Einstein's general theory of relativity, but they didn't get the name we know today until the 1960s. Karl Schwarzschild developed the idea for black holes from relativity's equations in 1963. David Finkelstein, in 1958, first published the interpretation of 'black hole' as a region of space from which nothing can escape."[1]

"*My, My!*" echoes everyone.

Jacqueline tags the moment with, "We know we are safe if we are getting the hum sound/vibration from Newton."

They are now traveling faster than light. That complicates things because of how navigation relies on light signals. They had just edged over the speed curve and were at 210,756.76 miles (about 339180.13 km) per second. Faster than the speed of light.

---

[1]. Lohnes, Kate. "How Do Black Holes Really Work?". *Encyclopedia Britannica*, 4 Jun. 2021, https://www.britannica.com/story/how-do-black-holes-really-work. Accessed 28 November 2024.

49

"Among the issues in play are mistakes in maintaining parallel universes," Kelly continues. "There are accounts—let us call them legends—that the Universe is matter and anti-matter. In science, we have what is known as 'CPT symmetry'; also known as 'CPT theorem, charge-parity-time symmetry'. Or, what is on the right is the same on the left, except they do not recognize each other. They do not exist one to the other, but they are in fact real. Occasionally something from one side finds its way to the other side and has no idea where it is. If that 'something' has cognitive ability—like a person—or advanced Artificial Intelligence (AI), we have a case study."

"*Whoa!*" comes as interest and alarm command attention.

No one in the group saw this kind of stuff in Kelly Marie. Yet, it made sense. Kelly was the one person who had the full attention of Merrilee. Kelly was the Tiffany member who could sit with Merrilee as 'Bastet.' Slide down on the floor with her as she groomed her ears, licked her paws, and snapped her tail. Merrilee knew all along who Kelly was. The starseed shapeshifter was tactically on top of her game. In the search ahead, it would be Jacqueline making command decisions based on Kelly Marie's ratification. Merrilee had collected her own Golden Chariot in these two women. Everyone was completely gobsmacked at the emerging reality.

A grand sigh of relief came from Solomon and Muhammad. Same with Aquinas. Sun Tzu, Che, and Hildegard were more circumspect. At this point, Jesus would believe anything, and John—as Lucifer—was a clear reminder of Thomas Hobbs and his equalizing power monster.

But, regardless of the overall mix—conflicts aplenty—this crew had cleared the hyper star, accelerated to beyond the speed of light, and were finding their way into the Quantum Enigma of good and evil.

Che could not help but ask his own fundamental question, "What are we going to do in the face of the enemy?"

Sun Tzu immediately faced Che. *"I came 544 years before Christ. I was, and may remain, the strategist of war. I was the mentor to Napoleon, Mao Zedong, General Douglas MacArthur, and you, my dear Che Guevara."*

Che stood silent as Sun Tzu continued.

"With The Art of War, *Emperors throughout time saw me as the underpin of their masterpiece. I taught them how to win whilst courting defeat. In this moment, I do not see the way of Sun Tzu as much as I see the way and discipline of the Samurai. Not my culture. I understand, however, we are not going on strategic field maneuvers here. We are going to encounter situations without notice. There is no field of battle here. We are travelers in the unknown Universe. We are more than Napoleon and the others. We are the advance of man's relationship with the cause of our very existence. And our almighty power starseed is telling us, as she told Thor and his gods of Mt. Olympus, that her strategy is 'Love.'"*

Sun Tzu finishes with the flash of his sword and the flourish of his celebrity . . .

"That situation, my dear travelers, requires us to have the discipline of the Samurai."

50

Everything was too new for an established routine. Tiffany et al. are getting used to the isolation of no isolation. In moments, they were moved through 'deep space' at speeds beyond their imaginations.

Jacqueline, true to her station, gave the opening reality check. She did her professional TED Talk throat clearing as she stalled to adjust the phantom microphone in her ear, and began, "Ladies and gentlemen, (then clears her throat again) as we enjoy these opening moments of interstellar to deep space travel, I want us to understand that 'light speed,' although impressive, is like standing still in this environment. It is true we can shadow moving stars, exoplanets and so on, but supercluster galaxies are spinning at 30 billion light years across. There are 31.54 million seconds assigned to the Gregorian annual calendar. So, that 30 billion light year crossing alone is 6.664e12 years in Gregorian time. At that rate, we are a generational adventure. We will need children and grandchildren and great-grandchildren to keep this going.

"Further, I am not clear what we will find as terminal velocity. We will cover that later. So, at this moment, we are but fractals of time on the overall approach to Merrilee's waypoints."

Newton's voice opened over Jacqueline: "I would consider 'Superposition' as the alternative to conventional miles and/or kilometers per second."

"Oh my, it's time for Jacqueline the Wizard to step it up," John titters under his breath.

"That's putting us in the frame of quantum mechanics," utters Jacqueline.

"Little spinners, Jacqueline—spin up and spin down. It's the electron dance people dream of . . . ." As John pressures, Jacqueline's face is carefully nonplussed.

"Yes," Hildegard says, and clears her voice. "I like the idea of Superposition. Anything that brings us to a wave function becomes pure in all environments."

"Absolutely brilliant. Fully interesting," Sun Tzu announces in favor of Hildegard's position.

"Well, it's true." Hildegard begins smiling.

"What do we know of 'superposition' Writ large?" Jacqueline is now staging her demeanor to accommodate a quick calculation.

Kelly Marie is frowning at Merrilee. "Are you going to add any functional freedom to this, or just hide in the weeds?"

"It's a well-tested theory, Kelly. They don't need me. I like it!"

Kelly squints one eye . . . as Jacqueline questions Sun Tzu.

51

"Look carefully to the horizon." Merrilee's voice drifts softly into the group.

"If we were a monolithic group, we would transcend space and time and be on our way as a seamless extension of ourselves. But we're not. The decoherence of our personalities creates conditions. Look carefully at any perimeter you feel could be the horizon."

As the members begin looking up, around, and over one another, they notice the ever-so-slight shimmering dance of light as their focus extends outward.

"We are now commingling with our environment as an antigen. That means we are coalesced as a hypersphere. The photon flashes on the boundary represent our sphere perimeter as we go to the edge of time."

Then, Kelly does Kelly, "Who steers this hyper sphere thing anyway?"

52

Kelly—before she and John ran with the butterflies in the Arizona desert—was a peripatetic traveler. Her talent followed her, and she could thrive no matter where she traveled. Her curiosity and intelligence unmatched in creation. So, it made perfect sense that Kelly Marie would immediately call for the question—any question. Who are you? Who is in charge? And, in this case, who is at the wheel?"

Each in their own way knew Kelly was unusual. She was humble, vulnerable, emotional, loving, and inside any toxic atmosphere was the matrix of the digital mind. She could go long and be safe. She could go short and be effective. And she could read space-time energy by electromagnetic changes. If Kim Stanley Robinson had met Kelly Marie before the *Mars Trilogy*, he would have written the *Enigma of Creation* instead. With Kelly, inductive reasoning left its hat at the door. She liked the black crows; however, in her words, *"do not try and bullshit me into thinking all crows are black."*

Kelly Marie was the antithesis of the 'General Conclusion.' Sometimes Kelly would play first-century editor. She could carry the sway of Aristotle and the dialogue of Cicero.

Kelly Marie was the entangled pulse of the enterprise.

53

"We know we will need to be operating inside a Glass-z12 galaxy with 'lookback time' of +/- 13.6 billion years. The Spectrum observations will be coming from Merrilee, as required." Jacqueline is rubbing her eyes as she speaks.

Kelly, biting the tip of her tongue—a little bit out between her teeth—nods her head to Jacqueline like she is listening to the chef give the cook time for a Delmonico or ribeye. The Tiffany women are sequestered as a fundamental force of nature.

As the A-lister theologian, Aquinas is fascinated with the new nomenclature. *"I know we will be chasing the red shift value of 'z' throughout this adventure; however, might I remind us that the warp of time knows no quarter when it comes to our kinship chasing around looking for God—or, as you say, 'First Cause.'"*

The ease of Aquinas in his statement was reflected in the face of the crowd. As he continued, his weight of talent shone the moment he invoked the influence of the Scorpion. His Scorpion flashback penetrated everyone.

"Do we remember when I brought John to Heaven? Do we remember that time—the time when we were worrying about the drawdown frequency? The time when the power of God was being siphoned off as frequency drain; that all we had to do was solve the riddle in John and Che. Stop John's ability to let Kelly and Jacqueline bleed to ground as they powered up ever so high?

"Do we remember the Scorpion, taking John as his charge—as the protégé of the God of War? How this enigmatic John, even as a clandestine Lucifer, ran to the Scorpion for counsel?

"Do we remember that it was the moment of John's pushed hyper shot at Merrilee that killed the Scorpion? Are we capable of standing erect in the z12 environment with the stain of John?"

Everyone was quiet, reflective.

"Aquinas, I feel your impulse."

Merrilee, now walking toward him, was not levitating as a manifestation of her dimensional power. She was walking straight at him. She stopped, extended her hands and put her left arm on his shoulder—pulled him into an embrace. Aquinas fell into his emotions and began to cry. He missed the Scorpion so.

As both adjusted, Merrilee leaned back, smiling.

"Aquinas, just so you understand, z12 in the spectrum represents 33.2 billion years—about 300 years before the First Cause. Classical physics in a quantum mechanics mix."

Her revelation stunned Aquinas. She released her hands from his shoulders and turned to the group.

"All of you, to the person, are important. We are on the most challenging mission in the history of time. You may have heard me say that before. If not, listen now. Each of you is a selection of one operating as a collective. Your purpose—singularly and severally—is timeless."

Then she turned again.

"I miss the Scorpion too—very much, Aquinas. Please stay with us in spirit, Doctor Angelicus, San Tommaso D'Aquino. Your 'Five Proofs of God' are in play."

54

Hildegard was animated in their new membrane environment.

"For centuries, I have been waiting for now. For the moment when we confront the hubris of God—his etymology with arrogance ; his failure brought on by his pride."

Solomon, Muhammad, and Aquinas were hit by her admission.

Sun Tzu was not.

"I guess this is as good a time as any." Sun Tzu was now fingering a copy of *The Art of War.*

"My experience living before Christ was without the scribes of Bible facts modifying my life. Not all of you have that advantage. There was a time when simulations ran in parallel with base existence. For valid reasons, most of you believe you are in truth. You believe firsthand in your presence in time and space."

Merrilee was instantly edgy. Sun Tzu was running in the slumgum of his past. He went on.

"Our Starseed Princess of NGC-234 is a simulation."

"Holy Shit." Che Guevara vomiting his words repeatedly, "Holy Shit!"

John was dead-still. Still like a cat on a kill. He looked at Merrilee. Her unease building by the second.

"It is not true, what Sun Tzu says here! It is not true!" comes from Merrilee.

By now the fear of betrayal has enveloped everyone. Each member is standing alone in fear.

Muhammad raises his arms. *"Strike him dead, Merrilee! Strike Sun Tzu dead if he says the falsehood of evil."*

Merrilee is flummoxed by both. She knows she has the power but there is no path. The words are frightening to everyone but to eliminate Sun Tzu? After all, she cannot kill him. He is already dead. This is not an option.

John lets out a long exhale. "You motherfucker! You're doing it to us, aren't you?"

Sun Tzu smiles at John. *"Yep,"* as he grins.

"You are a crazy, demented cockalorum. You are beating me at my own game."

Then John scans the group as he laughs and laughs. Merrilee, now more relaxed, realizes she is vulnerable to a rogue player. A quick time out of control notion from the crowd could spin the whole affair upside down. Figuratively, anyway. She motions to both Kelly Marie and Jacqueline to join her. As Kelly Marie moves in, she asks Merrilee, "Are you ok?" Merrilee smiles, "Yes."

Jacqueline gauges the crowd, looks at Sun Tzu, and smiles. "I'm coming for you, Sun Tzu." She smiles again.

"In your dreams, Jacqueline." The two of them helped relax the tone for what Jacqueline was about to say.

"Listen up, people. What just happened is not fantasy. There is much to unpack here, but in context the Universe can simulate itself just like a virus. We forget sometimes that we are in a complex environment. The starry, starry night around us is anything but simple. The Universe has built in optimization. Let us call it 'a God trick for protection.' And it makes no difference who you are, you can be a target. The difference is mass. Real has mass. A simulation has none. We must be computational in our existence. So, the short story is what just happened to us can, and will, happen again.

"Sun Tzu and Kelly Marie are working on another 'Osborne.' 'Katana Samurai,' they call it. Our plan is to protect ourselves in every way we can. We, of course, will keep you advised. Any questions?"

"Is there a back-side fix once a simulation takes ahold?"

"Not as yet that we know. We are front line players going forward. We must get this right on the pitch. There are no balls or strikes."

"I didn't know Jacqueline liked baseball."

"*Me either.*"

Che smiles at Aquinas as he swings his imaginary bat. Then he stops. "Wait a minute. Samurai!?"

55

As Che was focused on his own observation regarding Samurai, the Tiffany three were walking away in a chat about the fantastical properties of the Universe. It wasn't lost on Merrilee and company that Hildegard's original intent was going to be monumental.

The mix of people was interesting in itself—some dead, some alive. Traveling in a membrane for protection smacked of more pedestrian space travel. But there was ample evidence in science that the Universe was conscious of itself and interlopers on the wing.

Science as such was not in anyone's wheelhouse—save Kelly Marie and Jacqueline. The reality was setting in for the ancient few that there was stuff outside the solar system. Therefore, left to their own devices, they were already in Heaven. Game Over. So where's God?

Merrilee was the amalgam of every position. The gods of Egypt were replete with power options. In that environment, with her father Ra, she was acquainted with the acceleration of fiction toward fact. Not the case here. They were traveling in a doppelganger universe. Multiple reoccurring realities from all directions. The environment was more about astrophysics and metaphysics. In the Earth's solar system, metaphysics played a poor second to the hard science of astrophysics. In deep space that changes.

Merrilee knew that out here there is no need for alchemy. There is plenty of knotty stuff to go around. As she moved with NGC-234 and made her way through Andromeda, she ran headlong into black holes, quasars, Neutron stars, cosmic radiation, exoplanets, and the anomalies of gravity. She was seasoned by her own experience.

Jacqueline and Kelly Marie were studied in their approach, honoring Merrilee's experience. They knew what they had in Merrilee, but they didn't quite know what to do with the scope of what they had.

The mission was in a dichotomous relationship between new and established. Every member was chosen for singleness of strength. Also, maturity. Time-in-Grade. To Kelly Marie's original question, the ship did not need steering. The membrane became the will of the dominant member. A thought experiment at the highest level. The introduction of micropolitics was predictable. As the members floated past, what each saw in the face of the other was important for civility. But cheeriness and stupidity could be indistinguishable. There were arguments to be made, challenges to mount, and God to find.

Che had not moved. He knew that Merrilee sent Kelly Marie and Jacqueline to see Minamoto no Yoshitsune as the mission was in its final departure stage. Che raised his arms again, curled his hands in memory—holding a curved, slender, single-edged blade below the long grip guard.

"Samurai," he said again.

56

"I hate to bring up the word 'colossal' in the face of our power, but our operational space on this trip is outside the parameters of our cognitive ability."

"Is Aquinas saying we cannot think big enough to do this thing?"

"That's what it sounds like to me."

Jacqueline and Kelly Marie parlay Aquinas's words.

"Okay, Aquinas, try this. Nothing you see is in real time. We are living in the past at the speed of light. For all we know, the galaxies burned out light years ago and no mass exists anyway."

"Then why do we care about any of this?"

"Was that your position at the Committee table, Aquinas?"

"No."

"Okay then, we are in a no-see-um game of chance."

"Stop whining."

"New General Catalogue positioning is Pisces under—Andromeda over—and we are passing in 5, 4, 3, 2, 1 Execute."

Newton's words were spontaneous but rang like Mission Control. As the black sky began to flash stars past the membrane, Merrilee stood hard-fixed on the Star clusters of Pisces and Andromeda. Earlier they had left Andromeda and the House of Cepheus. Now, using a mirror-symmetrical parabola Nav-Trak . . . a U-shaped gravity slingshot brought them back for the final acceleration out. Over her shoulder she could hear John's voice, "Want to wave goodbye to your dad, Merrilee?"

Merrilee stood stone cold—billions of miles away from John's words. Ra was many things, but he was the father she needed after Lucifer's Hyperstrike.

Now, the course of 30 million light years of star clusters was a top-tier light show for sure. It staggered everyone's imagination. It also reminded the Tiffany three that without utilizing superposition, this trip was going to last forever, and ever and ever . . .

57

The validity of the membrane was environmental. Newton seemed to reside in that matrix—the membrane body politic with cognitive ability. Like a sheet of plastic wrap that formed up as a ball and said "Good Morning" when someone entered the kitchen.

There would be sensations and situations that were completely foreign to everyone . . . save Merrilee. And she was her own anomaly. Merrilee came from Pisces galaxy NGC-234—60 million light years from Earth. That meant, in perspective, the light seen on Earth from NGC-234 left Pisces 60 million years earlier. So, in their present moment of time, looking back to the Milky Way galaxy and Earth was 60 million light years in the past. For all they knew, Earth no longer existed—a thought not lost on Jacqueline and Kelly Marie, who had committed themselves to cross into the outer dimension if they could return to Earth.

It did not seem to make much difference the measure, the speed of light was restricting the viability of the trip. Unspoken but very real to the mission. True to the oddity, the membrane was influenced by Merrilee's thought process. So, no tradition there either. The membrane/Merrilee relationship was becoming René Descartes' "Cogito, ergo sum".

The Beings inside the arms of Newton must prepare to become electromagnetic waves. Merrilee had the demonstrated ability to get that done but she was the only one. To that end, Jacqueline had to address the gauzy antiquity of Aquinas, Solomon, and Muhammad. Aquinas continued to resurrect his case for First Cause action and reaction. In her mind, the daisy chain snipe hunt of all time.

None of this was adding up to "easy."

Newton broke everyone's thought process with: *"One of the intrinsic properties of an electron is its angular momentum, or spin. It is an empirical fact that the x-spin of an electron can take only one of two values, which for present purposes may be designated +1 and –1; the same is true of the y-spin."*

Newton was not to be taken lightly.

As she turned away from watching Andromeda whizz past, Kelly Marie cleared her head and went to sit by Merrilee. Her first words: "What happens if the membrane breaks?"

"Well, we will begin to smell rotten eggs. That's what space smells like, you know."

"Really!?"

"Yes. But it's an easy fix. A bigger issue is we will not be able to hear each other. Nothing available to vibrate sound. It will be dead-silent."

"Whoa . . . let's do that right now."

"Why?"

"Cuz I am tired of listening to Che shout **Samurai** as he swings his imaginary sword."

58

Jacqueline pulls on her R. Lee Ermey 'Full Metal Jacket' and calls out, "Bring Jesus Christ over here, Aquinas. We need to talk."

Since the disclosure of who Jesus Christ was to humanity, the Devil, and history, he had been lying low in the group. Head down, low profile. Jacqueline motions for him to take a seat, which is always funny because there are no seats. Jesus smiles and adjusts himself accordingly—no seat but, a seat.

"So, Jesus, what a life you lived—on the run with your father while being at the disposal of Lucifer. That must have been so debilitating."

"Yes, it was Jacqueline. Yes, it was."

"Jesus, you are aware that this deep space mission is underway to establish First Cause—a true God. Some artifact of an actual Christ. Instead of a prophet who talked too much, pissed off the Romans, and managed to get himself killed in the process.

"Making sense, Jesus?"

"You are very unkind, Jacqueline. I had little control over Lucifer. I was his invented fraud. He was an Archangel."

"Okay, okay, Jesus, I will meet you one-on-one but that will not make you anything other than the self-serving fugitive you are.

"Let us start with your involvement in the High Holy Order as the elusive son of God. Was there ever a time when anyone gave you an indication of God's existence? A circumstance? A place? A sighting? A frequency? Anything at all?"

"No, and I do not have to take this from you, Jacqueline."

"So, your tantrums over being crucified and returning too soon were simply gaslighting the whole time?"

"Yes, but I have been repeatedly clear. I am sorry for what I did."

Solomon is watching with Hildegard and Muhammad.

"Jesus seems to be giving this up awfully easy, don't you think, Hildegard?"

"Yeah. Too easy. I wonder if Jesus is still shilling for Lucifer AKA John. Like, Jesus is caving in to keep the light off John."

"SHIT!" comes from Solomon. *"We might have a big problem right out of the box."*

Listening to the speculation, John swoops in on himself—manifests Lucifer—looks down and to the left and causes Jesus to squeak and quiver in position. The mind-numbing fear on the face of Christ ratifies the corrupt power of the Devil.

"Jesus Christ was never smart enough to shill for me! As far as I am concerned, this puny man is a marionette in my backstage trunk."

"Well, I guess that solves that crisis." Hildegard is less than circumspect over what just transpired, but that was, most likely, her way of defusing Lucifer.

Jacqueline leans into Jesus and whispers in his ear, "Get a grip, Jesus. You're becoming an embarrassment."

Then she straightens up and rolls the line of questions back in time.

"Jesus, were you ever aware of the magnitude of what Lucifer had in store for you and your father? Who, by the way, where is your father, anyway?"

Jesus is silent, stoic, looking beyond the membrane.

"Let me help you out here, Jesus.

"God, et al—your story, not mine—appears to Moses with the Creation news. Tells Moses that the whole of the Universe happened in six days. And Moses decides to draft the Book of Genesis. Have I got that right?"

"Yes."

"So that means that you and Lucifer had to be in some kind of a time dilation."

"What do you mean?"

"I mean that Lucifer had to be jacking you around in space-time to accommodate whatever story he needed in the moment. You became Lucifer's false flag—to wave as required—but with no supporting army. Except God et al. brilliantly spins the package to include a couple of primates who run around naked stealing fruit. That, becoming the social benchmark for every generation of schoolchild in history. And, of course, smite thee with punishment to follow.

"Punishment to follow becomes the elixir of power. Lucifer lets it be known that hanging around the temple Ziggurat of Ur is a nonstarter. We have this new thing called the 'promised land'.

"And it goes on and on and on! And the more it goes, the more believable it becomes.

"You guys had a franchise on the mind of man."

Jacqueline, Kelly Marie and Princess Merrilee. Jacqueline had spent decades mastering the intricate dance of commerce, strategy, and leadership—navigating boardrooms with the precision of a battlefield commander. She understood risk, calculated opportunity, and had honed the instincts necessary to lead. But the expedition to Heaven was unlike any venture she had undertaken. This was no mere conquest—it was a pursuit beyond wealth, influence, or legacy. It required a mind sharpened by experience yet open to the unknown.

Jacqueline

At her side stood Kelly Marie, a Euclidean genius whose grasp of mathematics transcended human history. Where others saw numbers, she saw language—the unspoken dialect of the cosmos itself. She had dissected time, mapped the architecture of dimensions, and shaped equations that bridged the void between certainty and the divine. She alone deciphered the celestial patterns that guided their expedition, threading pathways between the stars with a precision only mathematics could provide.

Princess Merrilee of Solana was beyond definition. She moved between dimensions as if they were mere thresholds, slipping through time, bending space—existing beyond Euclidean precision and business logic alike. Kelly Marie could quantify galaxies, chart their spirals, calculate their trajectories—but she could not measure Merrilee. And Jacqueline, ever the strategist, understood that power which could not be defined could never be controlled.

Kelly Marie

Merrilee hailed from NGC 234, a galaxy near the swirling arms of Andromeda—a creature of quiet wisdom and relentless motion, slipping between mortal comprehension and divine legend. Sometimes, she became a flashing Hyperstrike—an unfathomable force cutting across space and time. But always, she remained an enigma.

Jacqueline studied her with a seasoned gaze, knowing Merrilee's presence was both an asset and a risk.

"You exist beyond the equations," Kelly Marie murmured one evening beneath the constellations. "Beyond my calculations, beyond anything I can quantify."

Merrilee tilted her head, starlight catching in her eyes. "You see the logic of space, Kelly. I see the fractures of time."

Merrilee was neither a subject nor a guide - she was the unknown. And in the journey ahead, the unknown would be their greatest ally and most terrifying uncertainty.

Belief in higher orders has always existed on a shifting spectrum—absolute conviction at one extreme, absolute doubt at the other. In between lies a vast terrain of adaptation, a fusion of certainty and skepticism shaped by the human condition. To be indisputable, belief must be rooted in science, proven through repeated replication. Anything beyond that enters the realm of speculation—fluid, subjective, evolving.

Merrilee

Thus, religion and science remain intertwined in their pursuit of truth, bound together like opposing forces in a yin-yang balance. Inquiry stands on one side, anchored in evidence and data: notion, on the other, upheld by belief and interpretation. Each challenge reshapes and occasionally collides with the other.

This series offers another perspective—not an erasure of belief, but a reformation, a unification of ideologies. It confronts sacred institutions, gender bias, and the immovable structures of monotheism. Within its pages, a woman crosses a threshold long fortified against her presence, reshaping history as she does.

The pursuit of truth is never singular nor simple. It is a hunt—one requiring courage, intellect, and an unrelenting willingness to ask:

What is it that we truly seek?

John

Lucifer

Bastet. Bastet, ancient Egyptian goddess worshiped in the form of a lioness and later a cat. The daughter of Ra, the sun god, Bastet was an ancient deity whose ferocious nature was ameliorated after the domestication of the cat around 1500 bce. She was native to Bubastis in the Nile River delta but also had an important cult at Memphis. In the Late and Ptolemaic periods large cemeteries of mummified cats were created at both sites, and thousands of bronze statuettes of the goddess were deposited as votive offerings. Small figures of cats were also worn as amulets . . .

Britannica, The Editors of Encyclopedia. "Bastet". Encyclopedia Britannica, 15 Jul. 2024, https://www.britannica.com/topic/Bastet. Accessed 13 January 2025.

Thomas Aquinas. St. Thomas Aquinas (born 1224/25, Roccasecca, near Aquino, Terra di Lavoro, Kingdom of Sicily [Italy]—died March 7, 1274, Fossanova, near Terracina, Latium, Papal States; canonized July 18, 1323; feast day January 28, formerly March 7) was an Italian Dominican theologian, the foremost medieval Scholastic. He developed his own conclusions from Aristotelian premises, notably in the metaphysics of personality, creation, and Providence. As a theologian, he was responsible in his two masterpieces, the Summa theologiae and the Summa contra gentiles, for the classical systematization of Latin theology, and, as a poet, he wrote some of the most gravely beautiful eucharistic hymns in the church's liturgy. His doctrinal system and the explanations and developments made by his followers are known as Thomism. Although many modern Roman Catholic theologians do not find St. Thomas altogether congenial, he is nevertheless recognized by the Roman Catholic Church as its foremost Western philosopher and theologian.

Chenu, Marie-Dominique. "St. Thomas Aquinas". Encyclopedia Britannica, 1 Aug. 2024, https://www.britannica.com/biography/Saint-Thomas-Aquinas. Accessed 10 January 2025.

Che Guevara. Che Guevara (born June 14, 1928, Rosario, Argentina—died October 9, 1967, La Higuera, Bolivia) was a theoretician and tactician of guerrilla warfare, a prominent communist figure in the Cuban Revolution (1956–59), and a guerrilla leader in South America. After his execution by the Bolivian army, he was regarded as a martyred hero by generations of leftists worldwide, and his image became an icon of leftist radicalism and anti-imperialism.

Guevara was the eldest of five children in a middle-class family of Spanish-Irish descent and leftist leanings. Although suffering from asthma, he excelled as an athlete and a scholar, completing his medical studies in 1953. He spent many of his holidays traveling in Latin America, and his observations of the great poverty of the masses contributed to his eventual conclusion that the only solution lay in violent revolution. He came to look upon Latin America not as a collection of separate nations but as a cultural and economic entity, the liberation of which would require an intercontinental strategy.

Sinclair, Andrew Annandale. "Che Guevara". Encyclopedia Britannica, 18 Nov. 2024, https://www.britannica.com/biography/Che-Guevara. Accessed 10 January 2025.

Jesus Christ. Although born in Bethlehem, according to Matthew and Luke, Jesus was a Galilean from Nazareth, a village near Sepphoris, one of the two major cities of Galilee (Tiberias was the other). He was born to Joseph and Mary sometime between 6 bce and shortly before the death of Herod the Great (Matthew 2; Luke 1:5) in 4 bce. According to Matthew and Luke, however, Joseph was only legally his father. They report that Mary was a virgin when Jesus was conceived and that she "was found to be with child from the Holy Spirit" (Matthew 1:18; cf. Luke 1:35). Joseph is said to have been a carpenter (Matthew 13:55)—that is, a craftsman who worked with his hands—and, according to Mark 6:3, Jesus also became a carpenter.

Pelikan, Jaroslav Jan and Sanders, E.P. "Jesus". Encyclopedia Britannica, 15 Jan. 2025, https://www.britannica.com/biography/Jesus. Accessed 15 January 2025.

Muhammad. Muhammad is born as a member of the tribe of Quraysh and the clan of Hāshim. His hometown of Mecca houses an ancient and famous pilgrimage sanctuary, the Kaʿbah. Although founded by Abraham, worship there has over time become dominated by polytheism and idolatry. Muhammad's conception is preceded by a dramatic crisis: his grandfather ʿAbd al-Muṭṭalib narrowly fails to implement a vow to sacrifice his favourite son and Muhammad's future father, ʿAbd Allāh, an obvious adaptation of the biblical story of the binding of Isaac (Genesis 22). Muhammad himself is born in 570, the same year in which the South Arabian king Abraha attempts to conquer Mecca and is thwarted by a divine intervention later alluded to in sūrah 105 of the Qurʾān. Muhammad's father passes away before his birth, leaving him in the care of his paternal grandfather, ʿAbd al-Muṭṭalib. At the age of six Muhammad also loses his mother Āminah, and at eight he loses his grandfather. Thereupon responsibility for Muhammad is assumed by the new head of the clan of Hāshim, his uncle Abū Ṭālib. While accompanying his uncle on a trading journey to Syria, Muhammad is recognized as a future prophet by a Christian monk.

Watt, William Montgomery and Sinai, Nicolai. "Muhammad". Encyclopedia Britannica, 7 Jan. 2025, https://www.britannica.com/biography/Muhammad. Accessed 10 January 2025.

Sun Tzu. Sun Tzu (flourished 5th century bce) was the reputed author of the Chinese classic Bingfa (The Art of War), the earliest known treatise on war and military science.

Sun Tzu, a military strategist and general who served the state of Wu near the end of the Spring and Autumn period (770–476 bce), is traditionally considered the author of The Art of War, but the work is more likely to have been written early in the Warring States period (475–221 bce), at a time when China was divided into six or seven states that often resorted to war with one another in their struggles for supremacy.

The Art of War is a systematic guide to strategy and tactics for rulers and commanders. The book discusses various maneuvers and the effect of terrain on the outcome of battles. It stresses the importance of accurate information about the enemy's forces, dispositions and deployments, and movements.

Britannica, The Editors of Encyclopedia. "Sun Tzu." Encyclopedia Britannica, 10 Dec. 2024, https://www.britannica.com/biography/Sunzi. Accessed 10 January 2025.

Solomon. The Bible says that Solomon consolidated his position by liquidating his opponents ruthlessly as soon as he acceded to the throne. Once rid of his foes, he established his friends in the key posts of the military, governmental, and religious institutions. Solomon also reinforced his position through military strength. In addition to infantry, he had at his disposal impressive chariotry and cavalry. The eighth chapter of 2 Chronicles recounts Solomon's successful military operations in Syria. His aim was the control of a great overland trading route. To consolidate his interests in the province, he planted Israelite colonies to look after military, administrative, and commercial matters. Such colonies, often including cities in which chariots and provisions were kept, were in the long tradition of combining mercantile and military personnel to take care of their sovereign's trading interests far from home. Megiddo, a town located at the pass through the Carmel range connecting the coastal plain with the Plain of Esdraelon, is the best-preserved example of one of the cities that Solomon is said to have established.

Gordon, Cyrus H. and Stefon, Matt. "Solomon". Encyclopedia Britannica, 29 Dec. 2024, https://www.britannica.com/biography/Solomon. Accessed 10 January 2025.

Hildegard of Beingen. St. Hildegard (born 1098, Böckelheim, West Franconia [Germany]—died September 17, 1179, Rupertsberg, near Bingen; canonized May 10, 2012; feast day September 17) was a German abbess, visionary mystic, and composer. In 2012 she was proclaimed a doctor of the church, one of only four women to have been so named. She is revered as a patron saint of musicians and writers.

Hildegard was born of noble parents and was educated at the Benedictine cloister of Disibodenberg by Jutta, an anchorite (religious recluse) and sister of the count of Spanheim. Hildegard was 15 years old when she began wearing the Benedictine habit and pursuing a religious life. She succeeded Jutta as prioress in 1136.

Britannica, The Editors of Encyclopaedia. "St. Hildegard". Encyclopedia Britannica, 1 Jan. 2025, https://www.britannica.com/biography/Saint-Hildegard. Accessed 13 January 2025.

Michael the Archangel. Michael, in the Bible and in the Qur'ān (as Mīkāl), one of the archangels. He is repeatedly depicted as the "great captain," the leader of the heavenly hosts, and the warrior helping the children of Israel. Early in the history of the Christian church he came to be regarded as the helper of the church's armies against the heathen and against the attacks of the Devil. He holds the secret of the mighty "word" by the utterance of which God created heaven and earth and was "the angel who spoke [to Moses] at Mount Sinai" (Acts 7:38). The numerous representations of Michael in art reflect his character as a warrior: he is shown with a sword, in combat with or triumph over a dragon, from the story in the Book of Revelation (Apocalypse).

Britannica, The Editors of Encyclopedia. "Michael". Encyclopedia Britannica, 20 Dec. 2024, https://www.britannica.com/topic/Michael-archangel. Accessed 13 January 2025.

Thor. Thor, deity common to all the early Germanic peoples, a great warrior represented as a red-bearded, middle-aged man of enormous strength, an implacable foe to the harmful race of giants but benevolent toward mankind. His figure was generally secondary to that of the god Odin, who in some traditions was his father; but in Iceland, and perhaps among all northern peoples except the royal families, he was apparently worshiped more than any other god. There is evidence that a corresponding deity named Thunor, or Thonar, was worshiped in England and continental Europe, but little is known about him.

Thor's name was the Germanic word for thunder, and it was the thunderbolt that was represented by his hammer, the attribute most commonly associated with him. The hammer, Mjollnir, had many marvelous qualities, including that of returning to the thrower like a boomerang; it is frequently carved on runic stones and funerary stelae.

Britannica, The Editors of Encyclopaedia. "Thor". Encyclopedia Britannica, 13 Dec. 2024, https://www.britannica.com/topic/Thor-Germanic-deity. Accessed 15 January 2025.

Mt. Olympus. Mount Olympus, mountain peak, the highest (9,570 feet [2,917 metres]) in Greece. It is part of the Olympus massif near the Gulf of Thérmai (Modern Greek: Thermaïkós) of the Aegean Sea and lies astride the border between Macedonia (Makedonía) and Thessaly (Thessalía). It is also designated as Upper Olympus (Áno Ólympos), as opposed to Lower Olympus (Káto Ólympos), an adjacent peak on the south rising to 5,210 feet (1,588 metres).

Mount Olympus is snowcapped and often has cloud cover. According to Homer's Odyssey, however, the peak never has storms and it basks in cloudless aithēr (Greek: "pure upper air"; thus "ether"). Later writers elaborated upon this description, which may have originated from the observation that the peak is often visible above a belt of relatively low clouds. In Greek mythology, Mount Olympus was regarded as the abode of the gods and the site of the throne of Zeus. The name Olympus was used for several other mountains as well as hills, villages, and mythical personages in Greece and Asia Minor.

Britannica, The Editors of Encyclopedia. "Mount Olympus." Encyclopedia Britannica, 5 Nov. 2024, https://www.britannica.com/place/Mount-Olympus-mountain-Greece. Accessed 13 January 2025.

John Duns Scotus. The certainty of Michael the Archangel knowing God. Although he accepted some aspects of Aristotelian abstractionism, John Duns Scotus (c. 1266–1308) did not base his account of human knowledge on that alone. According to him, there are four classes of things that can be known with certainty. First, there white, knowable simpliciter, including white, statements such as "Cicero is Tully" and propositions, later called analytic, such as "Man is rational." Duns Scotus claimed that such truths "coincide" with that which makes them true. One consequence of his view is that the negation of a simple truth is always inconsistent, even if it is not explicitly contradictory. The negation of "The whole is greater than any proper part," for example, is not explicitly contradictory, as is "Snow is white, and snow is not white." Nevertheless, it is inconsistent, because there is no possible situation in which it is true.

Stroll, Avrum and Martinich, A.P. "epistemology". Encyclopedia Britannica, 17 Dec. 2024, https://www.britannica.com/topic/epistemology. Accessed 13 January 2025.

Karl Barth. In the Christian understanding of Christ as being one with the Father, there is a possibility that faith in God will be absorbed in a "monochristism"—i.e., that the figure of the Son in the life of faith will overshadow the figure of the Father and thus cause it to disappear and that the figure of the Creator and Sustainer of the world will recede behind the figure of the Redeemer. Thus, the primacy of Christology and of the doctrine of justification in Reformation theology led to a depreciation of the creation doctrine and a Christian cosmology. This depreciation accelerated the estrangement between theology and the sciences during the period of the Enlightenment. This was subsequently distorted into a form of materialism. On the other hand, some 20th-century dialectical theologians, among them Karl Barth, in opposing materialism and humanism sometimes evoked a monotheistic character that strongly accented the centrality of Christ at the expense of some cultural ties.

Torrance, Thomas Forsyth. "Karl Barth". Encyclopedia Britannica, 9 May. 2024, https://www.britannica.com/biography/Karl-Barth. Accessed 15 January 2025.

St. Teresa of Avila. St. Teresa's acknowledgement of St. Hildegard of Bingen to become "Doctor of the Church." Born Teresa de Cepeda y Ahumada in Ávila, Spain, the woman who would become the first female doctor of the church defied her father's wishes when she entered a Carmelite convent about age 20. Health problems left her disabled for three years, during which she prayed fervently. After her recovery, however, she stopped praying. In 1555 Teresa experienced a religious awakening, one that not only changed her life but also the soul of the church. She dedicated herself to reforming the Carmelite order, both male and female branches, and founded many convents and monasteries.

Ostberg, René. "Women of Faith: Meet the Four Female Doctors of the Church". Encyclopedia Britannica, 5 Aug. 2024, https://www.britannica.com/topic/Women-of-Faith-Meet-the-Four-Female-Doctors-of-the-Church. Accessed 13 January 2025.

Bartolomé de Las Casas. The Apologética and the Destrucción—To stop the sin of domination. Upon his return to Santo Domingo, the unsuccessful priest and political reformer abandoned his reforming activities to take refuge in religious life. He joined the Dominican order in 1523. Four years later, while serving as prior of the convent of Puerto de Plata, a town in northern Santo Domingo, he began to write the Historia apologética. One of his major works, the Apologética was to serve as the introduction to his masterpiece, the Historia de las Indias. The Historia, which by his request was not published until after his death, is an account of all that had happened in the Indies just as he had seen or heard of it. But, rather than a chronicle, it is a prophetic interpretation of events. The purpose of all the facts he sets forth is the exposure of the "sin" of domination, oppression, and injustice that the European was inflicting upon the newly discovered peoples.

Dussel, Enrique. "Bartolomé de Las Casas". Encyclopedia Britannica, 25 Nov. 2024, https://www.britannica.com/biography/Bartolome-de-Las-Casas. Accessed 13 January 2025.

School of Athens. The political theory of Plato's Republic is notorious for its assertion that only philosophers should rule and for its hostility toward democracy, or rule by the many. In the latter respect it broadly reflects the views of the historical Socrates, whose criticisms of the democracy of Athens may have played a role in his trial and execution for impiety and other crimes in 399. In one of his last works, the Laws, Plato outlined in great detail a mixed constitution incorporating elements of both monarchy and democracy. Scholars are divided over the question of whether the Laws indicates that Plato changed his mind about the value of democracy or was simply making practical concessions in light of the limitations of human nature. According to the latter view, the state of the Republic remained Plato's ideal, or utopia, while that of the Laws represented the best that could be achieved in realistic circumstances, according to him.

Pulimood, Steven. "School of Athens". Encyclopedia Britannica, 11 Dec. 2024, https://www.britannica.com/topic/School-of-Athens. Accessed 15 January 2025.

Monotheism. Monotheism and polytheism are often thought of in rather simple terms—e.g., as merely a numerical contrast between the one and the many. The history of religions, however, indicates many phenomena and concepts that should warn against oversimplification in this matter. There is no valid reason to assume, for example, that monotheism is a later development in the history of religions than polytheism. There exists no historical material to prove that one system of belief is older than the other, although many scholars hold that monotheism is a higher form of religion and therefore must be a later development, assuming that what is higher came later. Moreover, it is not the oneness but the uniqueness of God that counts in monotheism; one god is not affirmed as the logical opposite of many gods but as an expression of divine might and power.

Baaren, Theodorus P. van. "monotheism". Encyclopedia Britannica, 9 Dec. 2024, https://www.britannica.com/topic/monotheism. Accessed 15 January 2025.

Gates of Paradise. Gates of Paradise, the pair of gilded bronze doors (1425–52) designed by the sculptor Lorenzo Ghiberti for the north entrance of the Baptistery of San Giovanni in Florence. Upon their completion, they were installed at the east entrance.

Each wing of the Gates of Paradise contains five large rectangular reliefs of scenes from the Old Testament between frigerated borders containing statuettes in niches and medallions with busts. Their format differs completely from the traditional medieval quatrefoils of the other doors. The original doors were restored early in the 21st century, and they are now in the Museo dell'Opera del Duomo; replicas adorn the entrance to the baptistery. The classically modeled figures within the reliefs are placed in landscapes or in perspectively rendered architecture to suggest a greater depth to the reliefs than actually exists. The 10 relief panels are among the greatest works of Early Renaissance sculpture. They demonstrate that Florentine artists had mastered linear perspective and the classical idiom by the early 15th century.

Britannica, The Editors of Encyclopedia. "Gates of Paradise." Encyclopedia Britannica, 11 Feb. 2020, https://www.britannica.com/topic/Gates-of-Paradise-by-Ghiberti. Accessed 13 January 2025.

Adam and Eve. In the Christian New Testament, Adam is a figure of some theological importance in the Pauline writings. Paul sees Adam as a forerunner to Christ, "a type of the one who was to come" (Romans 5:12). As Adam initiated human life upon earth, so Christ initiates the new life of humanity. Because of the sin of Adam, death came upon all. Because of the righteousness of Christ, life is given to all. Thus, in Paul's theology, it was Adam's sin and not failure to observe the Law of Moses that made the Gentiles sinners; therefore, Jews and Gentiles alike stand in need of the grace of Christ.

In later Christian theology, the concept of original sin took hold—a sin in which humankind has been held captive since the Fall of Adam and Eve. The doctrine was based on Pauline Scripture but has not been accepted by a number of Christian sects and interpreters, especially among those Christians who consider the story of Adam and Eve less a fact and more a metaphor of the relation of God and man.

Britannica, The Editors of Encyclopaedia. "Adam and Eve". Encyclopedia Britannica, 17 Dec. 2024, https://www.britannica.com/biography/Adam-and-Eve-biblical-literary-figures. Accessed 13 January 2025.

Pioneer Membrane Flyers. In 1987 British entrepreneur Richard Branson and Swedish aeronaut Per Lindstrand, aboard the Virgin Atlantic Flyer, made the first transatlantic flight in a hot-air balloon. And in 1991, aboard the Otsuka Flyer, they made the first transpacific flight in a hot-air balloon. In 1984 American aviator Joseph W. Kittinger, aboard the helium-filled Rosie O'Grady's Balloon of Peace, made the first solo transatlantic balloon flight. In 1995 American adventurer Steve Fossett, aboard the helium-filled Solo Challenger, made the first solo transpacific balloon flight.

Piccard, Donald L. "balloon flight". Encyclopedia Britannica, 25 Oct. 2023, https://www.britannica.com/technology/balloon-flight. Accessed 10 January 2025.

NGC234 & M31. Andromeda Galaxy, (catalog numbers NGC 224 and M31), great spiral galaxy in the constellation Andromeda, the nearest large galaxy. The Andromeda Galaxy is one of the few visible to the unaided eye, appearing as a milky blur. It is located about 2,480,000 light-years from Earth; its diameter is approximately 200,000 light-years; and it shares various characteristics with the Milky Way system. It was mentioned as early as 965 ce, in the Book of the Fixed Stars by the Islamic astronomer al-Ṣūfī, and rediscovered in 1612, shortly after the invention of the telescope, by the German astronomer Simon Marius, who said it resembled the light of a candle seen through a horn.

Britannica, The Editors of Encyclopedia. "Andromeda Galaxy". Encyclopedia Britannica, 11 Dec. 2024, https://www.britannica.com/place/Andromeda-Galaxy. Accessed 13 January 2025.

Interstellar Medium. Interstellar medium, region between the stars that contains vast, diffuse clouds of gases and minute solid particles. Such tenuous matter in the interstellar medium of the Milky Way system, in which the Earth is located, accounts for about 5 percent of the Galaxy's total mass.

The interstellar medium is filled primarily with hydrogen gas. A relatively significant amount of helium has also been detected, along with smaller percentages of such substances as calcium, sodium, water, ammonia, and formaldehyde. Sizable quantities of dust particles of uncertain composition are present as well. In addition, primary cosmic rays travel through interstellar space, and magnetic fields thread their way across much of the region.

Britannica, The Editors of Encyclopedia. "interstellar medium". *Encyclopedia Britannica*, 1 Oct. 2024, https://www.britannica.com/science/interstellar-medium. Accessed 9 January 2025.

Black Hole. Black hole, cosmic body of extremely intense gravity from which nothing, not even light, can escape. A black hole can be formed by the death of a massive star. When such a star has exhausted the internal thermonuclear fuels in its core at the end of its life, the core becomes unstable and gravitationally collapses inward upon itself, and the star's outer layers are blown away. The crushing weight of constituent matter falling in from all sides compresses the dying star to a point of zero volume and infinite density called the singularity.

Britannica, The Editors of Encyclopedia. "black hole". *Encyclopedia Britannica*, 3 Jan. 2025, https://www.britannica.com/science/black-hole. Accessed 10 January 2025.

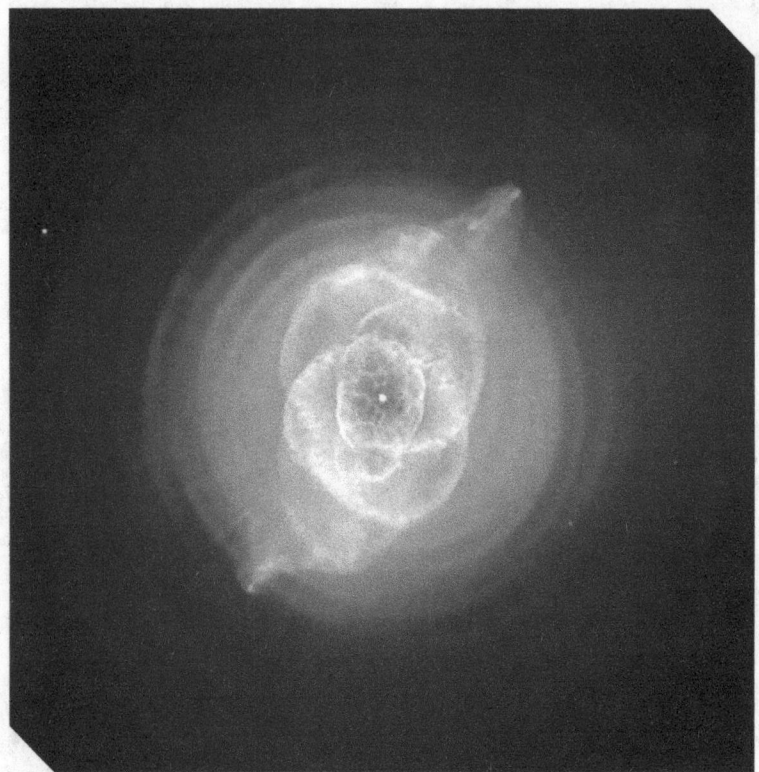

Cat's Eye Nebula. Nebula, any of the various tenuous clouds of gas and dust that occur in interstellar space. The term was formerly applied to any object outside the solar system that had a diffuse appearance rather than a point-like image, as in the case of a star. This definition, adopted at a time when very distant objects could not be resolved into detail, unfortunately includes two unrelated classes of objects: the extragalactic nebulae, now called galaxies, which are enormous collections of stars and gas, and the galactic nebulae, which are composed of the interstellar medium (the gas between the stars, with its accompanying small solid particles) within a single galaxy. Today the term nebula generally refers exclusively to the interstellar medium.

Mathis, John S. "nebula". Encyclopedia Britannica, 21 Aug. 2024, https://www.britannica.com/science/nebula. Accessed 10 January 2025.

"Here is where it falls apart, Jesus." Jacqueline is remaining in character as the inquisitor of Christ.

"Lucifer and you were convinced the story was solid—that no matter how it would spin, the outcome would be in your favor. What you missed was the confabulations of the mind of man. From 1380 AD to 1611 AD ten versions of the Story came into play. As palimpsests scraped deeper in lectionaries, we find that money corrupts, and power corrupts absolutely. Now as the 'Bible,' the story became the playbook of control over Christianity, Judaism, and Islam. All competing for a slice of the pie."

Lucifer, as he listens to Jacqueline's inquiry of Christ, is thumbing a Latin manuscript. From nowhere it seems. Then he stops. Looks to his hands. Raises his arms and throws the translation papers at Jacqueline.

"Stop, Jacqueline! Just Stop! Jesus Christ is not the enemy here."

Jacqueline backs away from Christ. She stares directly into the eyes of Lucifer. Her stare burning into the tablets of his brain. Lucifer knows Jacqueline to be a worthy master. A dab hand indeed. A woman who speaks above 38,000Hz. He knows she can position in the pitch of darkness. He will not challenge her. Lucifer bends down to retrieve the manuscript. Shakes it off. Straightens the pages. Acknowledges Jacqueline's gravity and says, "It's a push."

Jacqueline has Kelly Marie nearby.

"I loved him once you know."

"I know."

61

"Anyone here ever floated the Snake River to the Columbia?"

"What?"

"I said, anyone here ever floated the Snake River to the Columbia?"

"What, Kelly? What is that about?"

"Okay, Che, how about this. Have you looked closely at the surface of Jupiter?"

"U-mm . . . yes, I have."

"What did you see?"

"You can't see the surface because of constant swirling storms of Hydrogen and Helium."

"My point. Thank you."

"What point?"

"Come over here, Che. Look here—right here in the General Catalogue. We are right here."

Kelly's finger is coursing a line across a crease toward the upper right side of the page.

"Now, look over here on the continuing page, right around here."

All her fingers now splayed along the margin. The ambient light of deep space is beginning to dim.

"Now look here in the index."

She pages until she gets to 'pressures' and holds the page to the dimming light. "See that pressure index beyond M31 NGC- 234?"

"Yes. And?"

"Che, not to be condescending, but does the urgency in my voice give you any pause?"

Solomon and Muhammad lean in around Che.

"What's going on, Kelly?"

"Well . . . ever heard of monkeys in a barrel, Muhammad?"

"No."

"Okay, I get that. Of course you haven't. Solomon, would you call everybody over here. We need to address this quickly. We are about to get our teeth kicked out.

"I apologize for the metaphors and temper," says Kelly Marie, as she rapidly fingers the pages in the New General Catalogue.

Merrilee stands by quietly analyzing her crew.

62

"What we have is AR3234 developing into an X2-class solar flare. I am seeing it in multiple wave lengths and confirming with the General Catalogue projections I've been discussing with Sun Tzu.

"Navigation over the next time frame will be critical. We must come out of this with humor and dignity rather than beleaguered space travelers."

Kelly Marie's laying down the foundation for what was to come was weary in context. The search for God was not represented to be fight or flight around X2 solar flares, but the pressure gradients predicted violent outcomes in the near term.

There was a stationary feeling coursing through everyone. 'What to do?'

That feeling evaporated in nanoseconds as the membrane took a quick carnival spin.

"We are in it!" rang out from Kelly Marie.

Everything about this trip was orientation. There weren't the expected ricocheting gear problems of normal human flight. Flying objects were mostly nonexistent. With these Beings, the problem was maintaining angle orientation in a + speed of light package being warped around in entropy by radiation.

Jacqueline took Merrilee by the shoulders. "Have you got this?" as they spun around.

"No."

That was not what Jacqueline expected to hear. The hemostatic differences between Kelly, Jacqueline and all the rest were dynamic . . . dead and alive as it were. The radiation wind outcomes would be different. The bulk of the crew would be able to sustain limited equilibrium. Kelly and Jacqueline would go to dead short—their brain synapses would crash under the combination of pressures.

Kelly Marie was reaching, trying to get a hand on anything. Then she began to laugh aloud as she saw Solomon and Hildegard upside down; their bodies in funerary relief. Solomon in simla and Hildegard with a scarf around her neck.

"You two look like gauzy Octopi hovering over a shipwreck."

The membrane would adjust—stop and begin again. Kelly knew she needed a solution to stop a 4-axis rotation.

63

Che was holding his arms high as the membrane answered the pressure of the X-2 flair. Then he spun fast as his arms tried to follow the move. He stopped, raised his arms again, jacked himself straight, and shouted *"Uukahi!"*

He looked down, pressed two fingers one to the other, ran them up about 30 inches from his beltline. Like he was cleaning a blade. He shouted again. His spins were in counter rotation to the membrane. It was like he was reliving something in his past. In this moment, he was aware of X-2—completely aware.

Che's moves were of the Samurai. The raise – the balance – the swing. He would meet the X-2 pressure against the membrane with arms held high, then as the environment began a spin, Che would counterswing and shout. He was Waki-gamae, then Gedan-no-kamae. His rotating stance was of a Samurai with katana and wakizashi.

The membrane was answering his sword swings. His shouts. They were talking—arguing maybe. But Che Guevara was not in the jungles of Bolivia. He was in his head somewhere with Thais of the Ayutthaya Kingdom. It would be a 12th century military cast that tamed the storm of X-2.

Merrilee and Jacqueline were still holding on to each other. Both with eyes on Dr. Che Guevara. Kelly was fist pumping to his moves and shouting "Bushido, Bushido!" as the dance continued.

Jacqueline looked back at Merrilee. "I guess a Solar Flair and Feudal Japan are also 'a push.' Merrilee knew exactly what she meant.

As the environment slowed, Che slowed with it. Smooth, long sweeps with his arms, holding an imaginary katana. Che swung to a stop as did the membrane. They were away from X-2 enough to stand down.

"Still got your teeth, Kelly?" rang across everyone's space. Nobody would admit to its origin.

Merrilee, still with Jacqueline, raised the question of gravitational collapse.

"The problem, as I view this, will be avoiding a Schwarzschild radius to end up in some singularity."

Jacqueline let go of Merrilee's shoulders.

"I think you should address everyone right away, Merrilee. Do not . . . I repeat. Do not layer them up with the fear of a Schwarzschild radius."

Merrilee agreed.

Che remained oddly animated, eyes wide like he was displaced, to just return. He seemed confused. Kelly Marie caught his attention.

"Want to go with Jacqueline and me to see Minamoto No Yoshitsune?"

64

Che looked at Kelly Marie. Merrilee looked at Che. All three looked at Solomon, who asked, *"Do you know why we must isolate our search patterns?"*

"Why?" was universally returned.

"Because we are operating in infinity. We are in Zeno's Dichotomy Paradox. It takes infinity to chase infinity. We are not infinite. We are players within infinity. We can never be fast enough to catch the edge of the Escher space. So, 'First Cause' is the turtle in the Paradox. We will never find it, or God, or Brahma or whoever, if we try to simply catch the entity of First Cause."

In the same unison, the next question became, 'what do you suggest?'

"Well, Aquinas has the Summa Theologica *and his 'Five Proofs of God.' He is our best doorway into an intercept with God as First Cause. Aquinas has already isolated, in* Summa, *categories that will narrow the search."*

Jacqueline turns back to Merrilee. "What do you think of Aquinas taking a lead on this?"

Merrilee turned to face everyone.

"I believe we *are* the portal into a new realm. We, by our actions, define and inspire all who see our light. Therefore, we have the obligation to be the '*bright white light*' people need. I say that in the electromagnetic sense as well as philosophically. I have no issue with anyone doing what they do best. Or trying to do what they feel is best. We are a team of Occam's Razors. The Universe is under threat of incursion and eruption and though we are in deep space, this cloister is our world. We are the salvation of man, and we are underway. So, my answer is 'Every hand to their best approach, quick is the word and sharp is the action."

After an eternity of silence . . . came "Wow! Absolutely incredible."

"That was nothing short of electrifying!"

The radiation from X-2 had accelerated them to 511,790.458 meters per second.

65

"Ya know, Merrilee is smart. Surgically smart!"

"*What do you mean, John?*"

"Her short speech is what I mean."

"*It was good—no?*"

"Hell yes, it was good. Her quickie peptalk speech was straight out of *Master and Commander: The Far Side of the World*."

"*No kidding?*"

"Yeah, it was Captain Jack Aubrey during the Napoleonic Wars who said:

'England is under threat of invasion, and though we be on the far side of the world, this ship is our home. This ship is England. So it's every hand to his rope or gun, quick's the word and sharp's the action.'

"And, my dear fellow, she picked that right out of the Interstellar; modified accordingly, of course, because you can bet your ass she hasn't read *Master and Commander*."

John was standing over Aquinas, bearing down on him like a hawk looking at a field mouse.

"So, anyway, Aquinas, we're going to start using the *Summa* as our playbook?"

"*Looks like it.*"

"Going to be interesting—watching Tiffany scramble inside the bubble."

Kelly Marie is listening, and interrupts. "I think he will build his own Lion trap; Lucifer is going to try and beat the Dichotomy in the Paradox."

Aquinas and Lucifer stare at Kelly. Lucifer looks harder.

"You little rainy-day cupcake. Who the fuck do you think I am?!"

Kelly is stunned, but not stopped. "You are the antithesis of good, John. You are a self-absorbed has-been afraid of losing power. You are black mold. There is not a grain of good anywhere in your mix."

Lucifer raises his right arm, then hand toward Kelly Marie. The sheer force of nature flexed, with shots of lightning. A spectacular reminder of an earlier time.

The expression of luculent stood between them. The Scorpion. His curved stinger forward almost to his lateral eyes. He was arched and clicking. His trochanters were positioning his claws. A full spectrum corona rested across the environment.

Lucifer dropped his arm and hand.

Kelly grinned with a full smile.

The Scorpion moved into decoherence and was gone.

56

It's becoming clear that spontaneous leadership comes natural to the starseed. Jacqueline and Kelly Marie are not thrown into a muse over Merrilee, making this triad an effective management wedge. The obvious chink coming from John as he spotted Merrilee's capacity in front of the group. It wasn't that she could give an inspirational pep talk. It was that she could draw from resources heretofore unimagined by others. So, once again comes the obvious question: Who is she?

Lucifer the Archangel. Merrilee the what? 'Starseed' seemed a little thin. Starseeds were like hummingbirds. Bright, colorful projections of nature. Merrilee was more a Cooper's hawk on the fence waiting for lunch.

All the rest were ad hoc to the Tiffany.

Aquinas marshaled his charges for a look at *Summa Theologica* and his reactive explanations of God. The membrane was flashing through deep space at astounding speeds, and with an Aquinas grid system superposition might not be necessary.

A productive operation could become interstellar. Tenuous, for sure, but the intermingled clouds of gas—hydrogen with helium, ammonia and formaldehyde—could show anomalies from activity. Sort of a contrail from the pipe of God. Scientists had been measuring anomalies with instruments on Earth for over a hundred years. Why not here with a group of Beings who studied God's style and habits. Ticks in cosmic rays might be the breadcrumbs to First Cause. Background radiation might be the platform map for the Aquinas grid system.

The idea being to get out of the gas and into the golden orbs of actual Heaven. Not the contrivance of deflection Lucifer put together with Christ. The elaborate and insidious lunch table bureaucracy where John got sold to the Devil upon entry. The place where women became pathologically dependent on men in perpetuity.

Hildegard of Bingen and company were ready to play. She agreed in concept that God may be closer than previously thought. No need to run for the fences when God plays just as well among the bases in the infield. Hildegard was, once again, the baseball metaphor.

But the overall question remained among the members: Who was Merrilee? Could she be a Roald Dahl 'Irregular?' Are they stuck with an immensely intelligent mix of grace and intrigue?

If they do find God and /or First Cause, what will she really do? Maybe she is an assassin. Maybe there is an underlying friendship with Lucifer that trumps the most vivid fiction. She has the power to check every box. If this turns out to be espionage, how will it show? Who is Merrilee—really?

67

Aquinas is standing with Sun Tzu discussing the prototype, Katana Samurai.

"You know, Aquinas, Kelly and I made the Osborne with scrap U.S. Forest Service parts. This thing is not so easy."

"I'm not completely surprised, Sun Tzu. Early in the make-ready for this trip, I had a feeling there are forces working against us. The Universe is full of power franchises that—and, probably, who—want to protect their territory. I ran into that problem from my father, my own family. So, if someone, say you, are moving in on the power influence of a Dalai Lama or a Desmond Tutu, your road ahead is not going to be easy. If God is the target, that word travels fast.

"It's a man's club, Sun Tzu. Women need not apply."

"So, what you're saying, Aquinas, is that an implied cosmic structure protects the status quo?"

"That's how I see it, Sun Tzu."

"That means that we're not going to be able to build our Katana Samurai for protection."

"You are partly correct. But think about the alternative. Think of what happened as we went through X-2. Che Guevara was a full-on Heian shogun. No device necessary. Just focus and concentrate. I understand Che was a jungle fighter, but his X-2 performance unilaterally saved us from extinction."

"We have a Sisyphus task ahead of us, Sun Tzu, but I feel that somewhere in my Five Proofs, we will succeed."

"Tell me about that, Aquinas."

"I know we are looking for the First Cause. And I know my thoughts are medieval in today's science. However, as we both just remarked, there is an unseen power against us. No amount of modern science can do a proof of concept without a hard evidence sample.

"So, my medieval thought experiment is as good as the competition.

"I believe Lucifer is our shadowy player, working against us, just as a matter of his twisted principles. Merrilee, on the other hand, is not. She is the head of our spear. And our unseen enemy knows who she is, even if we don't. And I, along with the others, believe her complexities have the adversary scared. Real scared!"

"Yes, Aquinas, I can see your position, but God is the target?"

"Yes, he is. And maybe through no fault of his own. Lucifer has probably been gaslighting the pearly gates for at least two thousand years.

"God may have no idea how truly corrupt is his information. Especially if Lucifer's storyline is finding its way to the High Holy Order—I mean the real one. Not the invention we've been living in.

"Therefore, you see, Jacqueline, Kelly Marie, and Merrilee resemble the force of Charlamagne, the King of the Franks. We are carrying the female version of a Warrior King, except in our case, she's a Queen. Our Tiffany three becomes the polyglot of change in Heaven. They will speak to the power in whatever voice necessary."

"Wow, Aquinas. Impressive thinker you are."

Aquinas shrugs. "Yeah, it's good to shake off 550 years of dust. Under the Jesus Christ façade of Lucifer, none of my scholarship mattered."

"With that in mind, let's talk about my Five Proofs of God."

"Ok, go."

"Tradition has them as arguments, not proofs. In my thought experiment, Aristotle was correct about efficient cause. We must have movement from the beginning—First Cause, if you will. A sculptor cannot just look at a block of stone to succeed in art. He must place his chisel and strike it with his mallet."

Kelly Marie has been listening from up against the membrane and calls for the question:

"I love your simplicity, Aquinas. I'm wondering, have you ever heard of nematic chisels, or Minecraft real world LEGO bricks?"

"No."

Kelly smiles. "Ok, mind if I sit in?"

"No problem, Kelly. Have a seat."

68

"Aquinas, you are describing your Second Cause. Your First Cause has to do with the argument of motion, not action."

Kelly Marie nails her argument to his forehead—figuratively anyway.

Aquinas lets out a long sigh. *"Dammit, Kelly, you're right. That's never happened before."*

"It's the fog of war, Aquinas. It's got us all as we move into Merrilee's arena. The fear of the unknown. That even sounds funny considering who we are and where we are. But it looks to me like the yin yang of power never changes. Up or down it's the same. Must be a universal law that keeps all things in balance. We do not get a pass because we are interstellar travelers."

"So, Aquinas, which of your Five Proofs do you want to play across the cosmic background radiation grid?" Sun Tzu is manifesting a grid map in front of them.

Aquinas looks closely.

"Let's go with (diagonal -1/10) (ΛCDM model), 13.787 ± 0.020 billion years.

Observable universe: 8.8×1026 m (28.5 Gpc or 93 Gly)[4]

Mass (ordinary matter), At least 1053 kg[5]

Average density (with energy), 9.9×10-27 kg/m3[6]

Sun Tzu looks back to Aquinas with . . . *"Hmmm, really?"*

Kelly looks at both and says, "Switch to Deep Field. I want to have a look before you engage the grid."

160

Aquinas and Sun Tzu look at Kelly. She looks straight back. "Just do it, boys."

Kelly was much younger than either of the men, but she was smarter in orders of magnitude. Not one. Many. Sun Tzu moved his hand to indicate Deep Field. When the deep field came up on the screen, it was 2.6 arcminutes on a side. About 1/24,000,000 of the sky frame.

"What do you see, Kelly?"

"Hmmm, well . . . think of it this way. In context, I'm seeing a tennis ball at 100 meters. However, let's expand the frame and isolate on galaxy."

Sun Tzu complies with Kelly's ask.

"Do you see that—like a string—across the lower left quadrant of the frame?"

"Yes," from both men.

"Do you suppose that could be a tear in the fabric of space?"

Kelly Marie was demonstrating why she was visiting faculty at the Max Planck Institute. But more than that, she was giving a demonstration of how they were going to find God.

Merrilee, and Jacqueline, and Solomon, and Che, and Muhammad, and Hildegard, and Jesus Christ were in a half-circle around the three. Merrilee and Jacqueline moved in closer. Looked closer. Looked very closely—squinting.

"Are you sure, Kelly?"

"No, but what do you have that's better?"

Jacqueline pauses, then says, "That's too far at our track speed. Look for, maybe, some fabric tears closer and let's go have a look."

The cycle was broken. They were on the point and in the hunt. Their collective orientation was on the table—on the map—in the cosmic background radiation.

Aquinas was smiling. They were using his plan. But he couldn't help himself.

"Do we want to cover 3, 4 and 5?"

In that moment, Merrilee felt elated and empty for Aquinas at the same time. Aquinas just weathercocked the entire mission to align with his studied background. And, yet, in his insecurity, he felt a need to reach for more. She was sad in her starseed way. This old man had just set the map for the mission while being up against his own systemic barrier. His feelings of invisibility, and frustration, were on his sleeve, and no one seemed to notice.

69

The environment was unusually warm as the membrane passed through Nebula gas. Risky business in some cases; however, the operational side of Tiffany was some of the remote interconnection of Merrilee that Jacqueline must work with. Merrilee enjoyed Jacqueline's aspect. The bottom line for Merrilee was Jacqueline's flawless history in business and her humor in adversity. She was quick in action and measured in her decisions. When Jacqueline said the words "Let's go have a look," Merrilee knew they were in play.

That reality ignited an observable change in Merrilee. She seemed uneasy. Jacqueline saw the change immediately and took Merrilee aside.

"We are in this together, Merrilee. You, me, the lot of us. In spite of all my experience, I'm scared. My sense is you are as well."

Merrilee reached a hand to Jacqueline.

"Thank you. It's easy to have conversational bravado when speaking of God—of the power of Creation—the dynamism of 'God save the King or Queen,' but we are, as never before, barbarians at His gate."

"That's precisely what everyone has been asking: Who are 'you', Merrilee, and, what are we doing?"

"A long time ago" . . . Merrilee started to smile . . . "that sounds like a bedtime story, doesn't it?—the energy of Creation was the amalgam of existence. It was the whole cloth of the universal consciousness. That was the fundamental mystery. The mystery of mysteries, if you will."

"Yes, I believe that."

"Then, in the process of evolution—call it natural selection—differing immersive processes began to simultaneously attack the core of the High Order metaverse."

"Ummm . . . what does that mean, Merrilee?"

"The modeling platform was under attack. The First Cause plan was jumping the rails. If there was a plan, an original plan, it was in trouble.

"At the time, I was a Seraphim in repose. There were many of us. We were all in the immersive evolution of the Core Being, but we never knew what 'Core Being' meant. That went on for millennium upon millennium. We were being suspended, as space-time moved forward."

"Holy shit. How old are you, anyway?"

"I really don't know." Merrilee began to laugh. "I've been around for one 'hell-of-a long-time' . . . don't tell anyone I couched my answer that way. I'm supposed to be better than that."

Jacqueline smiled in acquiescence.

"Anyway, eventually I was assigned to the Milky Way galaxy. To Earth. To Egypt. I was given to Ra, the Sun God of Egypt. I was to bring him the power of the Sun."

"You have that kind of power!?"

"Yes, I do, and more. Twenty-five thousand suns, it's been said."

Jacqueline remained quiet. She had heard this before, but now she was stunned by the reality of power at her side. Then she asked, "Barbarians at His gate? What does that mean, Merrilee?"

"Hildegard of Bingen was the first to recognize the bias of Heaven and how that bias marginalized her existence. She and Thomas Aquinas scouted me out. They knew of me through Ecclesiastic history.

"They knew the Seraphim of Heaven as a powerful cloister. We operate independent of all else. We are the original 'Irregulars.' As a cloister member with immense power—some from Ra—my new assignment was to place the High Holy Order in decoherence. Destabilize it, I guess is a better phrase. There were two gender orders in the original Heaven. They were referenced in what was to come, first, as scripto continuum. Eventually known as the Bible. But therein resides the problem. The Bible became a reflection of bias. Of men over women. There was no effort made to change the paradigm. In The Old Testament—the first

Books of the Bible—the abuse of women was legion everywhere. And that carried forward. The New Testament Books were better, but the damage had been done."

"So, Merrilee, with all your power and history, why haven't you just kicked down the door of Heaven and walked in?"

"Because the High Holy Order knows I'm coming. The change happened when we were under the crush of Mars. You remember that, of course."

"Yes."

"During that space-time, Jesus Christ came out as a double agent of the Devil. We had no idea that was afoot. I'm sure you remember that as well."

"Yes."

"Everything changed. Lucifer was outed by his own man. Christ gave it up. That sent alarms throughout space and time. But only to a point. The overriding question: Did God know or had Lucifer deceived God in his villainy?"

"What I'm hearing, Merrilee, is we are at war with Heaven and Heaven might not know it?"

"Essentially, yes."

"The unknown is how many false flags Lucifer has flown."

"We know Lucifer has made all of Creation to believe I am the danger. I am the new Gates of Hell. I am the reincarnation of Dante's Inferno. I am the Hell Hound at their heels."

70

With their mission refocused on finding a tear in the fabric of space, all the elements of wonder and adventure were highlighted. As a unit, Tiffany and company were an incredible force. At light speed ++ its mass, albeit small, any anomaly off the track moved some from weightlessness to being slammed against the membrane. Then the adjustment to microgravity as the position adjusts—then weightless again.

The mix of people types—that being both dead and alive—changed the gravity influence on mass. Under pressure, Jacqueline and Kelly got tossed around like steelies in a pinball machine. The rest of the complement was unphased. This oddity wasn't wasted on developed humor throughout. Jacqueline could be talking to Solomon and in a slight +/- pressure moment be tossed through him to ricochet off the membrane sidewall. He would then turn around and keep talking like nothing happened.

The same problem in sleep. Kelly and Jacqueline would tie one another to a fastening so as not to float away. All the rest either didn't sleep—no need—or just closed their eyes to refresh some track of uninterrupted thought.

Moment to moment in the membrane was a combination of excitement and routine. Decidedly different from Earthwise space travel wherein equipment and technology carried out the mission. Smoke and rocket fuel and shaking and exploding if something went wrong.

Sun Tzu and Aquinas continued to calibrate the cosmic background radiation grid to find tear targets. That became a "tt" acronym for their job category. Sun Tzu and Aquinas doing 'tt' seemed to satisfy the inquisitors among the crew.

The naysayers questioned the value of a clandestine entry through a tear in space-time fabric. "Why not just show up for a sit-down with God? Maybe just arouse God's sympathy for change."

Lucifer laughed to himself as he listened to the conversations. He mused, "That would be like showing up unannounced at an Old Man's private club insisting that there were to be no more cigars, naked women, or whiskey."

71

Among the challenges facing Tiffany and company was one hiding in plain sight: universal consciousness. Merrilee did not discuss this with Jacqueline earlier, but she was acutely aware of its impact. On the surface, everyone was blaming Lucifer for what went wrong. Easy to understand. Underlying that was the Universe itself. The matter-of-fact substances that played to the arenas of the cognitive and inert.

The Metaverse of the Universe dealt in sextillions of bytes. Merrilee didn't see the need to obfuscate her travelers with the thought experiment to visualize the operational side of a billion gigabytes times a thousand every twelve seconds.

In the soup of deep space, the data/datum was not filtered out, it was filtered forward. That meant to Merrilee that her movements were being monitored by the Beings she was going after. She was the fish, and they held the bowl.

Merrilee had at her disposal the collective of her fellow minds. But they were as vulnerable as she if nothing was done to subvert the eye of God. Merrilee's time in Egypt under the 'Eye of Ra' provided operational experience. Would that be enough in the so-much-to-register environment?

It was unavoidably obvious that the diversity among members would distort the learning curve inside the membrane. The question: Was there strength in variety? The scholars among them operated in theories. Merrilee and Jacqueline needed facts. Merrilee spoke to Jacqueline. She quickly understood the situation. They were under the eye of cosmic consciousness and needed to somehow slip away.

As Jacqueline faced outside the membrane, she was deep in thought. She turned to Merrilee and looked at her. Merrilee was wearing a smile.

"What's the smile about, Merrilee?"

"I just finished reading *Master and Commander: The Far Side of the World*."

"What? When?"

"A few minutes ago."

"How long have you been wetting your beak in Napoleonic history?"

"Wetting my beak?"

"Never mind. When did you start reading Patrick O'Brian's series?"

"A few minutes ago."

"You started a few minutes ago, and now you're done."

"Yes."

"You read *Master and Commander* in a few minutes?"

"No, I read *Master and Commander* and *Post Captain* and *H.M.S. Surprise* and *The Mauritius Command* and *Desolation Island* and *The Fortune of War* and *The Surgeon's Mate* and *The Ionian Mission* and *Treason's Harbour* and *The Far Side of the World* and *The Reverse of the Medal* and *The Letter of Marque* and *The Thirteen-Gun Salute* and *The Nutmeg of Consolation* and *Clarissa Oakes* and *The Wine-Dark Sea* and *The Commodore* and *The Yellow Admiral* and *The Hundred Days* and *Blue at the Mizzen*."

"And you read these books in a few minutes?"

"Yes."

"I see."

Jacqueline was masking her face as she tried to imagine reading 7,000 to 10,000 pages of text in a few minutes."

"So, Merrilee, what did you think of the Aubrey-Maturin series?"

"I admire Dr. Maturin, and I think Captain Aubrey is exciting."

"And all of this in a few minutes?"

"Yes."

"Merrilee, do you know how big a sextillion is?"

"It's 1,000,000,000,000,000,000,000 bytes. Or 10 to the 21st power."

"I see."

Jacqueline turned away to look back outside the membrane. Her teeth were crunched together. Her eyes were blinking like an owl in high wind. She put her right hand to her forehead trying to smooth out the squint being etched into her skin.

Merrilee moved closer to Jacqueline and said, "I have an idea."

Jacqueline said, "Un-huh. I bet you do."

72

Jacqueline turned to rest against the membrane. Merrilee, still smiling. The reality check Merrilee just provided was lost in the moment. She had an idea. That was a first for Jacqueline. Merrilee had always been a purveyor of the command decision. 'I am this and/or that', with limited historical reference.

Now, she simply steps out of the box with a casual piece of news that she read Patrick O'Brian's series on Napoleonic maritime history in a matter of minutes. Less than five minutes by gauging her remarks. Coursing through Jacqueline's mind is, "What else can she do?"

"What's your idea, Merrilee?"

"Well, in *Master and Commander: The Far Side of the World*, Captain Jack Aubrey and the sailors of the *HMS Surprise* were being chased by the French privateer *Acheron* off the coast of Brazil. Aubrey and his men were out-manned and out-gunned."

"Okay." Jacqueline is now in complete surprise at this new scholastic side of Merrilee.

Merrilee continues. "The French privateer fires a cannon at the *HMS Surprise* until she's dismasted with heavy damage. In that situation, Captain Aubrey manages to drift into a fog bank to be lost from the French."

"'*She's*' dismasted" . . . Merrilee?"

"Yes, it's a tradition sailors have. They spend so much time sleeping on their ships, they apply a feminine gender to these eccentric relationships."

"So, okay, Merrilee, I'm satisfied you are a walking AI supercomputer. What's your idea?"

"Well . . . Captain Aubrey . . ."

"We are back to Aubrey again?"

"Yes."

"Okay . . . go on."

"In the fog, the French privateer *Acheron* continues to hunt the *HMS Surprise*. Captain Aubrey knows that another encounter will cost him his ship and his men. So, he takes scrap material off his deck and builds a decoy."

"Like another ship?"

"Yes. Under the cover of darkness, Aubrey snuffs out the running lights on *HMS Surprise* and puts running lights on this raft kind of a thing. Then, lets it drift off in another direction. The French see the lights and end up following the raft. Aubrey gets away to rebuild his ship in the Galapagos Islands . . . and the story goes on."

"I see."

"Yes, I think you do see, Jacqueline. We are going to become the bird of many colors and send the "Eye of God" down a rabbit hole."

Jacqueline breaks into hysterics, bends over laughing even harder, and says, "Merrilee, you are the most interesting creature in the whole Universe. I just love you!"

Merrilee sniffs away laughing tears to look out and into the stars . . .

"That's the whole point now, isn't it, Jacqueline?"

73

Spinning around in Jacqueline and Merrilee's heads was 'method'. What will be the method for a clandestine entry through a tear in the fabric of space and time? By now Kelly Marie has entered the latitude around the other two. Her intuition tells her a plan is gestating. Merrilee recites another *Master and Commander* for Kelly and Kelly positions herself against the membrane as she calculates aloud. "5% ordinary matter, 27% dark matter, 68% dark energy."

"What's that about, Kelly?" in some derivative form comes from Jacqueline and Merrilee.

"That's the standard formula for total environment. I always start there. Think of it as spider webs in an abandoned closet—but everywhere. Simply everywhere we can imagine. Just EVERYWHERE."

"Yes, okay, we got that. It's everywhere."

"Yeah, but here is the spooky part. The mass of galaxies and the gravity of galaxies do not relate computationally. The galaxies mass should provide way more gravity, but this is not the case. So, we have this no-see-um stuff that distorts classical physics/astrophysics."

"Where are we going with this, Kelly?"

"We—and I say 'we' advisedly—are working with media we can't navigate because we can't see it. We are going to be in deduction navigation using induction thought. So, welcome to the fashion, faith, and fantasy universe, ladies.

What we do know is the times multiple of each we can measure with instrumentation."

Kelly Marie layers information on Jacqueline and Merrilee like she does at Max Planck or CERN. She is drop-dead smart. And everyone in the astrophysics community anchors on her for obvious reasons. She continues with tactical indifference. Not to Jacqueline and Merrilee, but to the whole idea of playing dice with the cosmos.

"This is not going to get easier, ladies, so let's move on. All this 'matter' I'm referencing operates in circles—halos more like it. The European Organization for Nuclear Research (CERN) calculates this stuff in space, on the surface of planets and underground on Earth, 24/7, and here is what they know, or think they know. Dark Matter—the 27% item—operates without regard to gravity. Dark Matter plays in the void of space and doesn't care about mass. Ya can't make this shit up . . . it's as crazy as it sounds."

Jacqueline looks at Merrilee and in her classic management style, says "Fuck!"

74

Jacqueline, making her thoughts clear with the usually obscene noun she picked up from John, defers to her statistical, social science and psychology background.

"We are going to move this into factor analysis. This is a 'principal component' problem. Our assumption should be that the Universe is conscious. We are impacted by the physics of the material when what we should be focused on is the step-by-step process of universal thought. In other words, the Universe thinks. The Universe matter Kelly described—the spider webs in the closet stuff—formats like a brain. And a brain formats like the Universe. And they both think."

Kelly Marie looks at Jacqueline. "Not bad, Jacqueline. Not bad."

Jacqueline smiles back, then twists her nose.

"Yeah, right. Don't think you can skate from cleaning the nebula fog off the membrane position moments. It's your turn and that's not changing just because you're trying to stick a little 'feel good' on my nose."

"I did it last week!"

"No, you went to sleep last week, and I did it for you!"

"I did?"

"Yes, you did, oh Max Planck / CERN genius."

Merrilee looks at Jacqueline and Kelly Marie. She just stands there looking at them. Finally, she responds, "I don't recall being prepped by any cosmic order for what I just experienced in the two of you. We are in a game of psychometrics. Why didn't I see that earlier? I don't know. But now I do. Thank you. Thank you both!"

Kelly Marie looks at Merrilee and Jacqueline. "Well, I guess that makes us a team."

Being set free from the purposeless dogma of hard science, Jacqueline and Kelly Marie, in their cohesive personality, have positioned Merrilee as the manifestation of cosmic consciousness.

75

As they quiet down, Merrilee is stopped abruptly by a felt strangeness. She poses a question to Jacqueline and Kelly:

"Is there an ontological difference among methods? If the Universe thinks, what might it think in interpretation? Have we just built our own destruction? If the Universe thinks, and if that thinking believes we are obtrusive, how do we know?"

"Not to worry, Merrilee. This is the reason we are here—Me and Kelly, I mean. There was something in your Being that caused your original decision regarding everyone here. That includes the two of us. You must go forward with the understanding that you are the chosen one. And, in that truth, who 'you' choose falls in line with your cosmic consciousness."

Kelly pushes back against the membrane. "That means *all* of us, Merrilee. Everyone in the membrane is in line with your frequency."

"Not so fast!" is the refrain from across the membrane. "*You three seem to be sucking your own lube oil. Like it's 'Us and Them,' according to you.*"

Jacqueline, Kelly Marie, and Merrilee do not advance an answer. And that situation is amping up the tension quickly.

Muhammad speaks into the void: "*We must understand the structure of things. That includes the Universe in total. All of us in the membrane are cherished by the Metaverse for differing reasons. It was Hildegard who felt her frequency in the beginning. And, yet she is not in the Tiffany we see before us. My belief is we are all 'First among Equals' in this enterprise.*"

Merrilee looks to Hildegard. As their eyes meet, the understanding becomes instantly apparent. There is nothing standing between them, figuratively or not. They are a unit. As Merrilee continues to measure the group with her eyes, every response is the same—absolute devotedness to the Being of both. And that worked until she got to John.

A long painful stare . . .

"You will betray me," she says.

76

The existential (Heidegger) erudition of "Being" didn't take the edge off Merrilee's belief that John would betray her. There was a felt rush from everyone as she put the words into play. It was generally unspoken, but understood, that John, as Lucifer, and Merrilee, the Deep Space visitor, had a conjunct of staggering power. A direct conflict between them became unthinkable.

Solomon stood to underwrite Muhammad's opening commentary.

"No great expedition has gone before us without conflict. And none of them had the potential for change like ours. And, I say 'ours' in earnest, as the collective we are."

That seemed to put an ease over the group. John and Merrilee were standing down. The membrane was doing hyper speed through the design of the Universe. For the membrane it was back-to-track and finding a tear in space-time large enough to put them on the "other side."

The enigma around a change of guard in Heaven hovered over everyone like a 1944 landing on Omaha Beach. Luck being more important than power. They would be going against the greatest command authority of the Universe in ways given to courting their own defeat. No cultivated relationships for support. No history of successful positioning. The attack stratagem was "Love," which didn't seem a fit with rampant hostility.

But all things intrinsically probable had a chance of success. It was the *scope* of the chance that had everyone scared.

77

"We see an open option at:

Right ascension, 14h 39m 36.49400s
Declination, -60° 50' 02.3737"
Apparent magnitude (V), +0.01
α Centauri B (Toliman),
Right ascension, 14h 39m 35.06311s
Declination, -60° 50' 15.0992"
Apparent magnitude (V), +1.33 . . ."

Sun Tzu rang it hard aloud . . . then he said it again. It rang the same way, piercing everyone. If there was homeostasis in this gang of souls, it would be a mess. His words were stunning to everyone; it was hard to believe. There was a tear at the right ascension large enough for a pass-through.

They had been coursing like a ribbon through space and time for this moment. Now a thin line to violence, butchery, sleeplessness and fear. No one knew.

What would be the God of Creation? The mental exhaustion was mind-bending. The men imagined a stealthy flanking to the heroic seizure of God. The women, a vast rolling plane of holographic images to infinity.

Kelly Marie said, "Check this, Sun Tzu. I think your right ascension should be 14 hours,. 40 minutes flat."

He did and she was right. Would have been a critical error if their trajectory was off by the first calculation.

"Okay, everybody. On entry start we need everyone against the membrane walls. Hard and tight. We have no time to lose. This is a valid target. We may not get another chance for a long time—if ever."

Merrilee was still in the middle, not on the wall.

"What about you, Merrilee?" from Hildegard.

"I'll be fine . . . not to worry. I will be fine."

Then Merrilee reached toward Kelly Marie. *"Do you remember our walk away from the collapse of Mars?"*

The starseed was like a dentist pulling a kid's earlobe before sticking a needle in the roof of her mouth. Their bodies silhouetted in white light, and they were gone.

78

As the membrane comes to rest, the interoperability of the space is not segmented as binary. It is bright, almost too bright—white. Good and/or evil have no evident representation. There is a sort of Fifth Avenue at noon rush of deities, saints, angels, souls, and venerated ancestors—all on the run to somewhere. There is what looks like a real-time nautical chart hovering over everyone with moving icons. Showing are two chart categories: "The Matrix" and "The Other."

The overall action is disturbing and hard to follow. There is a low rack of Head Mounted Displays (HMD) directly in front of everyone. A guy walks up to the old-looking member, Solomon, and asks . . .

"Do you have an advance directive or manifest?"

Solomon looks at him—stares at him—mouth open. Che Guevara answers for Solomon, "No."

Next question: "Are you all dead?"

Jacqueline answers over everyone, "Fuck No!"

Kelly burps and laughs.

The guy looks at Jacqueline and says, "Heaven has a 'Not Dead' visitors option."

"Excellent," says Jacqueline. "Where do we register?"

"We?"

"Yes, there are two alive. The rest are dead."

"Will anyone require optical waveguides?"

"*What's that?*" and the guy looks hard at Aquinas.

"'That' is the 'HMD' on your advance directive."

"*We don't have one.*"

"I didn't say you had one. It's on your directive. Wait a minute. You really don't have an advance directive?"

"*No.*"

"Where are you from, then?"

The guy lights up and shouts, "BREACH INFRACTION—BREACH INFRACTION!"

. . . Che pushes his forearm ulna into the guy's neck. The guy starts to choke. Che pulls the guy's head forward with a chop to the C-6 vertebrae on the base of his neck. The guy goes down. There is blinding light and defining clackers sounding everywhere. The whole place is a kicked ant hill of rush and panic.

Jacqueline leans into Kelly Marie. "Do you have a cigarette?"

"Ha Ha . . . Yeah, right. You don't smoke anyway."

"I do now."

79

Jacqueline was the first to open her eyes. She was followed by Che and Hildegard. They were in nothingness. It was quiet. Much like the first time Merrilee had them sequestered in a group on the way to Mt. Olympus. They looked in an arc and over each other. There was a sound now—faint it was. Like a sound that didn't care if it was a sound. Like it was singing to itself.

Merrilee was on her back. Quiet but awake. She kept looking straight up. Focused on something.

Aquinas sort of rattled his way to his knees, rosary draped on one arm as he struggled to stand. He turned to Che. *"Man, you really hit that guy hard, Che!"*

"What guy?"

"The guy who was asking us for our documents. Some sort of travel documents, I guess."

"What guy? What the hell are you talking about?"

"The guy who met us when we arrived. You were there, Kelly. You saw him."

"Nope."

Jacqueline looked at Kelly. "Did I ask you for a cigarette this morning?"

"What? WTF are you, no, we, talking about here? You don't smoke and neither do I smoke! And if I did it wouldn't be cigarettes anyway."

Merrilee rose from her waist, still sitting. "I saw what you're talking about, Aquinas."

"Okay, there, see? I'm not crazy. And Che just about killed that 'take our tickets' guy."

Che had no idea what any of this was about. Everyone stared at Merrilee as she posed a question to the group:

"I did notice that when asked for the body count, I wasn't included as dead or alive. Jacqueline made her 'I'm alive' demand and Kelly was included. Everyone else was dead. So, in the order of time, I am what?"

Most of the group didn't know what she was talking about. Aquinas did. *"That makes you kind of a mechanism, I guess. Undiscoverable, unless you want to be seen. A time traveler shapeshifter, spirit, goddess."*

"YES!" Che jumps in. "That's what she is all right. A time-traveling Doctor Who."

Merrilee looks at Che.

"If you're right. If I were a Doctor Who time-traveler, what would happen? Did it happen this morning? How did we land in somebody's ticket line?"

Everyone was attentive. Nobody answered.

"Get up, Che. Let me show you something."

Merrilee stands behind Che with her forearms on his shoulders. Then she slowly moves them off and out toward 15 degrees.

"Tell me when my arms disappear from your peripheral vision, Che."

She keeps moving her arms away from his shoulders. Away and away. Finally, they are out and about 25 degrees back of his line of sight. He still sees them.

"Okay, Che. You can sit back down. Thank you for helping me."

Merrilee gathered everyone in her visual scope.

"Do you all remember before we left, Kelly did a quick recalculation of position. A few degrees to flat, as I recall?"

"Yes," came the answer all around.

Then Merrilee turned back to Che as she posed her question. "Do we know what some scientists believe lies between 14 degrees and 25 degrees off a sight line?"

"What?"

"The frequency of the Multiverse. Part of the Many-Worlds Theory advanced by Sean Carroll at Cal-Tech in California. And I think we may have found it just for a moment. Kelly got us there in tiny degrees of freedom."

Merrilee was now calm in the conversation—listening.

The group excitement increased to "Wow!!"

"Quantum worlds and the emergence of space-time. And we were there. We were in the dizzying hall-of-mirrors. Maybe the first ever! . . ."

"So, where are we now, then?"

Merrilee asks Jacqueline and Kelly to join her. They paused to feel the environment. The slight sound from the quiet. The odd hue of a not-color spectrum but color nonetheless.

"I feel we are in the Metaverse. It's the electromagnetic frequency—top tier Seraphim version—the anteroom of Heaven, if you will."

Everyone was stone silent. A few hours earlier they were in a clown show of weirdness. Now, they were the Barbarians at the Gate. In reflection, how pitifully silly that felt.

"Che Guevara, what are you doing!?"

"I think I'm getting some harmonics from the sound."

Che was on Sun Tzu's shoulders reaching up while holding his arms in a circle. He resembles a radio direction finder left over from government surplus.

They are turning around like they were anti-aircraft radar in an old black-and-white war movie.

Suddenly, there is this head pressure of wind and thunder. Then lightning. Then a freakish kind of groaning like maybe a T-Rex fighting to get out of quicksand 30 million years earlier. Then quiet. Sun Tzu and Che were knocked flat by nothing apparent. Then, from somewhere:

"For the Lord himself will come down from Heaven, with a loud command, with the voice of the archangel and with the trumpet call of God . . ."

"Oh, my God!" squeaks out of Aquinas.

"What's the matter, Aquinas?" Hildegard moves in to hold him.

"*They know we're here!*" Aquinas cries.

"Who knows we're here?"

"The Guardians at the Gate."

Hildegard looks at Merrilee. "Aquinas thinks we've been found out. Says the Guardians are close, or they know we are here anyway."

Merrilee looks up. "I know."

As Merrilee acknowledges Hildegard, the whole environment becomes textured. Congenial. Alive. Everyone has a kind of shimmer. A full-spectrum glow. Quietly, the sound of heralding trumpets begins in Adagio. Faraway.

Merrilee is standing, head up. The trumpet cadence quickens—louder—into a high-order canon.

Merrilee remains standing. Fully aware. The environment seems heavy—to be breathing. Alive.

As Merrilee stands, she recites from Psalms: *"Be exalted, O God, above the heavens let your glory be over all the Earth."*

The group moves down around her feet and is utterly terrified.

18

"You are Princess Merrilee?"

"I am."

"I am Hachiman, the God of War. You are Bastet, the daughter of Ra?"

"I am."

"I bring you Benzaiten the Goddess of Knowledge and Arts. You have a member of the code of Bushido."

Merrilee hesitates. Che answers, "Yes, we do."

The voices seemed to be spontaneous from in front of Merrilee and the group. Che stood up and moved next to Merrilee. Side by side they looked up and forward.

"I am Che Guevara from the code of Bushido."

"Come forward, Che Guevara."

Che steps forward without hesitation.

"You are the Divine Warrior?"

"Yes, I am."

"You are of the Samurai code—loyalty, honor, and bravery?"

"Yes, I am."

None of this is happening face-to-face. The voice is from nowhere and Merrilee, now standing with Che, is accepting the dialogue, albeit confusing. Hachiman seems to be a gatekeeper. He obviously knows of Merrilee as 'Princess Merrilee,' and he was aware that there may be a Bushido coded warrior in the mix. His gift of Benzaiten in gender might be a gesture that there are important women in Heaven.

Also, none of the recited scripture is on the table. The first announcement about the trumpet call and the voice of the archangel isn't in the dialogue. Merrilee's answer to the exaltation of God, the same. Nowhere. Even more confusing is the dialogue players' names are from a Buddhist belief system.

Merrilee calls for the question.

"Hachiman, if I might ask, where are we?"

"Princess Merrilee, you are in the transmigration of the vertical continuation of Heaven. This place is for voyagers in the existential planes."

"So, we are not among the Golden Orbs of the Seraphim?"

"No."

Jacqueline spins . . . "Kelly! Kelly Marie!!"

Kelly jumps in close to Jacqueline.

"Kelly, we got to tighten up this track thing. I do not want to take another shot and end up with Tenzin Gyatso in Tibet."

Kelly agrees and starts to recalculate the track.

Jacqueline looks at Che. "What's this Bushido code stuff about?"

Merrilee sits down with the others. "That was interesting."

82

"Okay, listen up, everybody. We did a great job of getting through the tear in the fabric of space and time. Now we must figure out how to navigate around in here."

Jacqueline assured everyone that, although the last conversations with the imminence of Heaven were interesting, those kinds of sidebars do not fit the mission profile.

Kelly Marie, now refining her long-range markers for the next move, is head down in her navigation abstractions.

Merrilee, dancing with her own divine intervention, is concerned about the right response to whatever perplexing tone comes along from the Kingdom of God.

Aquinas is trying to stabilize against the reality that there is a God, and Che must now explain to everyone the Samurai story he fed Hachiman.

John brings his own set of facts regarding what they know. That the Christian experience is based on confabulations designed by Lucifer.

So, armed with these fact sets, they are going forward with caution. No support systems and one enemy within. John was curious to himself because of his unpredictable influence from Lucifer. A friend one minute and foe the next. But his Lucifer curiosity remained due to his archangel fight for power in Heaven. His loss being the driver for retribution.

Rising to the immediate top was Che Guevara as a Bushido warrior. Che was flushed knowing he was outed by himself. Always the wry-tongued cynic, he must now peel his own onion, with everyone watching as the layers came off.

"When I was executed in the jungles of Bolivia, I resurrected in the time dilation of the Kamakura period of Japan. Because of my fighter/revolutionary history, I was immediately placed before the Shogun. I was trained in the Warrior Caste of the Samurai, becoming a formal stoic Bushido. I ran in the Tokugawa shogunate. I was a Samurai in armor. Oddly enough, it was you, Aquinas, who took me away, again."

Aquinas was visibly stunned by this revelation.

"When Hildegard recruited you for what we have now, she, being a musician, was operational in a frequency shared by Zen Buddhism in Samurai culture. I was on that frequency at the same time. Probably a mistake. Nonetheless, I was taken up by the shared influence between you and Hildegard, and I was placed in another order. I became a fixture in the High Holy Order. And, what none of us realized was that same frequency was what ignited your interest in John. "We were both—through Zen—bleeding off the frequency of the power of God. And, to make it even more complicated, we came to find John as a double agent."

Lucifer stands in the group. "Amazing stuff, Che. You and John, I mean."

"The amazing stuff, Lucifer, is that as you stand there, I know you're John."

Kelly Marie rises to the situation.

"None of this is news to our Starseed Merrilee, it would seem to me anyway." She takes a laser look at Merrilee.

Merrilee, who is thinking of form, not fashion, stands for everyone.

"I am 'the one' in this bunch. And as that, I know who you are, what you are, and how you are. You are here because of a special property each of you has—your Being in Time. You are indeed favored and important. All your backgrounds are in play as required.

"Maybe, based on these Zen caste stories from Che, we can view it this way. You are the caste of skilled Samurai, and I am your Bushido Shogun."

"*A light year represents 5.8 trillion miles. I believe we will find God in that frame. No need to look further.*" Aquinas sounds convincing.

"What drives that conclusion, Aquinas?"

"*I don't know, Jacqueline. I just have a feeling.*"

Jacqueline smiles at Kelly Marie. "I can hardly wait to present that stratagem to *Scientific American*."

"*Sarcasm does not move us forward, Jacqueline.*"

Aquinas is upset over her sarcasm. Jacqueline moves between sarcasm and leadership.

"Kelly, how are you coming on a new set of coordinates for another shot at the High Order?"

Jacqueline runs her organization right out of a Wall Street playbook. In her world, a mistake is a termination. In this group, she must get used to the idea that nobody gets fired. Mistakes are acknowledged as opportunities for better, but no positions change. All the faces remain. What she does not miss, however, is Kelly's level of intelligence. For Jacqueline, or anyone else for that matter, a sit-down with Kelly Marie is drinking from the firehose of acumen.

"I know this feels like we are in the middle of a Fermi paradox, but I think I've found an anomaly to a secondary opening inside the original tear."

Kelly Marie is, once again, fingering her paper stack with Jacqueline close at hand. A carefully sharpened L&C, 5-H yellow, Koh-i-Noor between Kelly's teeth. Jacqueline knew Koh-i-Noor developed the drawing pencil in 1790 and she wanted one. Kelly was thinking about it. A game they both played.

Merrilee comes over to have a look. The membrane is uneasy in its positioning; feels drifty like it's not tethered. Kelly and Merrilee stabilize.

"I don't think there is any downside to this shot," says Kelly. "All we will be doing is returning to square #1 and we might fit into another track—right there."

Merrilee trusts Kelly to the core. She agrees to the shot. Kelly signals Sun Tzu to come over.

"I plan to take a shot in relative state formation. Going to do a 'Ready/Ready' Schrödinger spin."

Sun Tzu arches his neck up and forward. *"That gives you two options on landing. Do you want that?"*

"The way I see it, I give myself a mulligan. If I'm wrong, I can get out on the other side. Maybe we call it the 'Schrödinger (2) Cat Shot.'"

"I see the humor, Kelly. I hope you're right."

"This is going to be a six-billion-mile quantum entanglement. We will split the Universe as we go. You will see quantized electron orbits reminiscent of the Solvay Conference in 1927."

"What's she talking about?"

"Hell if I know."

Kelly stacked the amplitude oscillation—the environment split, there was a lightning flash, and they were gone.

84

Inscrutable was the takeaway from the '2 cat Schrödinger' shot. In nanoseconds, the shot split space and time as suggested, but not in the tradition of the 1927 Solvay Conference. Kelly was fighting her fingers as the influence of mass upon gravity was reversed. They were doing hyper speed in the middle of the fundamental weirdness of quantum mechanics. The situation was all epistemic theories gone bad.

Not one among them realized the pioneering going on. This Merrilee adventure was where no man had gone before. More importantly, in a space never breached by man. If Lewis and Clark were around, they would be cheering in the stands.

The cross mentorship of three women, along with the dynamical collapse of hidden variables, put this group in Poincaré motion in three space-time dimensions. They are uncomfortably close to the center of power.

There was no deception possible. Merrilee and company were now bracketed in the reticle of First Cause. If astrophysics' out-of-phase speculations were correct, Merrilee and Aquinas and all the rest were about to become vapor in deep space.

Never had there been such a thing. This was the source code. Nobody visited here! Merrilee knew they were bracketed in, with no escape.

Then, utterly wondrous reality clarified the situation.

They were standing directly in the gaze of God.

85

Jacqueline turns to Merrilee. "I think you should stipulate that what we have here is God."

"Yeah," comes from Che. "This could be just another obelisk in a secondary structure."

Kelly and Sun Tzu agree.

"If this is God, we should not be stuck in space-time. We should be able to look outside for some geometry. No decorated permutations of reality. We do not need a God that lives in our headsets."

Then Kelly Marie nails down the science parameters.

"Outside of space-time we find the obelisk empire. What we know is math prevails to a point. Two points in fact. For 'space', math is accurate up to 10 to minus 33 centimeters. For 'time', the accuracy comes apart at 10 to minus 43 seconds.

"Even if this is God, he is only God until we squeeze him down to minus millions of zeros . . . 399 million zeros to be more precise."

Aquinas reaches away from Kelly for anything normalized.

"Your implication is we may never know if this entity is God or not?"

"That's right. This could be another Lucifer and John gaslight adventure."

Merrilee, who is listening with quiet intensity and is thankful for the precision of her fellows, changes the perspective.

"Every theory begins with a miracle. The standard model of physics still needs perception that it cannot prove. It's 'perception'. We live in a panpsychist environment. We speak to science in spiritual tradition. We use experience to teach. The term 'God' is a spiritual tradition. Reality, i.e. God, is not nerve and sinew in your brain. God is the interstation of our experience. 'a' (interval) 'b' = God.

"I think a dog is a dog. I do not go around calling someone's dog a quadruped. When I sit among Red Oak trees, I am quiet as I meditate. When I return to friends who might ask where I've been, I do not say I've had a lovely afternoon with 'Quercus rubra.'"

She turns back around to face whatever the speculation. She asks for Aquinas to join her.

"Here we go, Aquinas. I would like you to tell God that you were appointed theological adviser and lecturer to the papal Curia, then the center of Western humanism."

Aquinas feels a personal victory from the bidding of Princess Merrilee. Never in his time among the Papal States had he been called by such authority.

He began:

"*My dear God of Gods, I am Doctor Angelicus, San Tommaso d'Aquino, born 1274 AD near Terra di Lavoro, in the Kingdom Sicily. I was canonized in 1323 AD. My theologiae mentor was Aristotle born 384 BCE, Stagira, Chalcidice, Greece.*

"*I give myself to you today as a medieval Scholastic. I bring to you the classical systematization of Latin theology. I am considered the foremost philosopher of Western civilization.*"

On hearing Aquinas, Jacqueline speculates to Kelly Marie, "I wonder what we do if God accepts Aquinas's offer and just sucks him up into dark matter?"

Their bilateral chuckle is real, but so is their concern. Merrilee, standing next to Aquinas, is stone still—watching for any sign. Still no overt signal from the God Particle or whatever is before them. Merrilee remains silent, allowing the intent of thrice.

Then it comes again. The same trumpets in Adagio. The same amplitude toward a High Order canon. Then the voice.

"I know you, Aquinas, and I know the woman next to you."

In this thrice, the group is, for some reason, not overwhelmed with irrational fear.

The expression of the voice continues:

"You, Princess Merrilee, are my faithful servant. You illuminate reason and quest for truth. It is you who inspires the heart and mind of man. It is your voice of reason that brings you to the divine. To your clarity. To God's spiritual depth."

Merrilee gestures to Aquinas and responds:

"It is Aquinas who understands the relationship between voice and reason.

I learn from him his *Five Proofs* of your existence in his *Summa Theologiae.*"

Sun Tzu leans into Che: *"Damn, she is so smart. Merrilee is not going to acknowledge his compliment. She is going to bait God right out of his box."*

"Yeah."

87

There remains no manifestation of God beyond voice. The environment is bright and fantastical. If Aquinas and Merrilee are standing in the epicenter of cosmologies, this experience is the antithesis of an antichrist. If they are in the host galaxy, and if the 'voice' is the host, they are standing in a 99.5 percent clean particle approach to God.

As this observation begins its transition to actuality, Sun Tzu and Kelly Marie take a mental deviation to what it would be like if the group were some other. Like, maybe, Niels Bohr, who would discuss his model of the atom with God. Maybe Albert Einstein, who would give God a chalk board example of the relation of mass to gravity. Marie Curie would stand with two Nobel Prizes draped across her shoulders and neck to explain how radioactive isotopes became the foundation for nuclear physics.

The situation in front of them was that something obtuse to expected reality had the power to swallow entire galaxies into **extension**.

And, Princess Merrilee reasoned her quarter under the cushion as she told God—the voice—to chalk his stick and take his best shot on the break. She smiled and racked the balls with Aquinas standing as her second.

In the moments that followed, the uniform smooth of the Universe came into play as conformal hyperbolic geometry. God was telling his visitor that to challenge him on the break was her fantasy. He was, who He was, and he controlled all the balls.

In the order of time, the game between Merrilee and the voice of God went on. It was like they both enjoyed developing Escher's uniform geometry, and either could run to the edge of time and never be caught.

The membrane group—to the person—was stupefied by Merrilee's acumen in her exchange with God.

As Merrilee and the voice of God dive in and out of classical prejudices, they both try to make their High Ground intellectualism as they spar with their own empiricism. There is a noticeable haphazard sprinkling of support as they trade cosmological invocations from the density of endless archangels and the secular gallery of Stephen Hawking, Werner Heisenberg, Michael Faraday, Niels Bohr, Erwin Schrödinger, Max Planck, and Paul Dirac.

In the opinion of Solomon and Muhammad, the entire sequence was becoming a case of who could support their argument by indexing the biggest names in the shortest time. Instead of ratifying the question of the unquestioned, Merrilee and the voice of God were having a playful, but serious, go at each other.

All of this was understandable considering Merrilee's willingness to question the distinguished physiognomy of the face of God. It was noticeable to senior Seraphim that never in the history of time had such scallywags popped into Heaven unannounced for a hold your own sit-down with First Cause, i.e., God. What was even worse—in the eye of the six-winged Seraphim she knew were hovering around God—she was succeeding. It was Hildegard of Bingen who caught Merrilee's attention long enough to change the paradigm.

"Merrilee, it's obvious you are obtaining the truth (to John, that's *gaining traction*) by subordinating your stack of arguments. All your positions contain the intellectual structure to prevail in kind. How about we just tell him why we're here?"

Merrilee was a bit crestfallen by Hildegard's comment. On the other hand, she could see from all around the perimeter that she was everyone's new-found champion.

From the beginning, Merrilee had been the accidental protector. That included Ra and all the women and children of Egypt. She had endured the collapse of Mars, the death of the Scorpion, and the Hyperstrike of Lucifer. But until now, she had never been tested at such a level. Her remarkable intellectual arguments in social science and quantum physics were substantial. By collaborating with her team, she knew she could be positioned to establish a beachhead in Heaven. An astoundingly positive opening gambit.

It was one thing to have a friendly spar with God. It was quite another to put him on notice that this array of stock was the inquisitor of his corps d'elite in social dynamics. Merrilee was concerned that right now wasn't the best timing. She instinctively understood that God was tracing their Fraunhofer lines for spectrum absorption changes. The universal High Holy Order litmus test. She had been in similar circumstances with Ra and the gods of Egypt. She did not want God to overreact to a potential threat.

"*Let's advise him in advance of the possible results on the Fraunhofer lines,*" Sun Tzu suggested as an alternative.

Merrilee liked the idea. "He will see the spectrum change in us but will not necessarily see a threat."

Suddenly, there is a thunderous laugh—like laughter cascading along limitless hallways. Then rolling thunder in crescendos of frequency.

"What do you take me for, you trifle of fools?" The voice was back.

Jacqueline passes her eyes over everyone with, "Well, that takes care of that."

Hildegard of Bingen stands erect in the face of God.

"I am your trifling fool, my dear God. I am the person of the idea. You, my Holy Father, are my target. These who are with me are my contemporaries in various disciplines. If you view them, your laugh will not be so robust."

Jacqueline turns to Kelly. "Signal everyone to get over here so we can form up as a wedge. Give this High Holy Order guy a little heartburn."

"That is 'God' to you, Jacqueline." His voice does a laser track through the tablets of her brain.

Che layers it up toward the voice with some of his 'revolutionary' bravado. "You, my dear First Cause pretender, are the inadequate burst of Gamma rays *en esta reunión*. You are nothing more than a dying star."

With incredible speed, the visible Universe is distorted in an optical afterglow. An unrecognizable spectrum frequency outside astrophysics. Then the light is amped up to a billion times brighter than 5778K—Planck's constant of the sun. Every concern of Merrilee's is instantly splashed across the visible spectrum.

Jacqueline shouts over the particles of disambiguation: "We are sorry, oh cherished *Ahura Mazda!* Please accept our apology and chagrin in this moment of ignorance."

Everything goes silent. The light spectrum returns to the standard model.

God looks at Jacqueline.

"You are wise, Jacqueline, with your invocation of Ahura Mazda."

Now back beside Jacqueline, Merrilee says, "How did you know what to say?"

"I just figured, if he is God, he will come in many forms. I picked the most obscure of possibilities and got his attention. Standard issue management stuff, Merrilee."

Merrilee winks. "Impressive."

Jacqueline winks. "And to you."

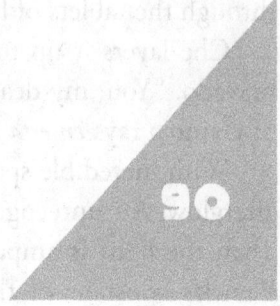

90

While open anxiety over an encounter with God had lessened in their ranks, nothing was predictable going forward. The voice of God dominated the environment. Merrilee had a successful one-on-one discussion of Canon law with the voice of God surrounded by High Order Seraphim. The six-winged Seraphim were the only bonafides they had, and that was supposition.

The 'Voice of God' was arrogant and dismissive. So, something was hidden in God's tone. Perhaps fear.

"How did this group breach the ramparts of Heaven with such ease?" must be the obvious question among members of the High Holy Order Archangels.

Merrilee and company were in a self-induced dichotomy over how to proceed. Che, being 'Che', was pushing for aggression. Aquinas, being the Scholar, wanted nonintervention leading to compromise. All the women seemed strategic. The Teddy Roosevelt approach—"Speak softly and carry a big stick." The stick being Merrilee.

The obvious lack of cohesion was working against a perceived model:. 'After all, Merrilee knows what to do.' The problem was, she didn't. So, Kelly Marie and Jacqueline were shepherding a 'secret weapon of love' with a sense of bewilderment over Merrilee's own perplexity. If they were, in fact, talking with God, nothing fit tradition. God acknowledged Aquinas and Merrilee, only to dismiss them as a 'trifle of fools.'

All this is a far cry from the old days of 'Floppy Feathers' when the 'Committee' in Lucifer's contrived Heaven was easy to calculate. Maybe there was something to "God created Heaven and Earth," and the Devil said, "Let me organize it for you."

The reality of today is classic Joan of Arc in the right nave of Notre Dame. The woman warrior enters the fight because of her belief in a First Cause parity of life. The fatal flaw here—God decided to write off women as a total loss. They were in a man's world that will, most likely, turn out to be Heaven.

91

As Jacqueline and Merrilee move to the edge of the membrane, Jacqueline takes their together opportunity toward structure.

"Ya know, Merrilee, we need an interoperable plan that is scalable to our changing circumstance."

"Okay . . . Hmm? You mean something that can't be contaminated by a singular predictive influence. Hmmm . . . How about we catalog a virtual identity of everyone into one piece of code. Something that updates the Matrix constantly. That way the cross-title assets will have a home in real-time. Maybe we develop this like a spatial game. Then we all jump into the portal design and tweak the digital physical connections. We put full sounds and textures inside the model so unreal becomes real. That way we can be anywhere, and our operational field looks the same."

"Ah ha, yeah, Merrilee . . . yep . . ."

Kelly was walking behind them to the membrane perimeter.

Jacqueline and Kelly Marie slowed to let Merrilee head toward Che for some clarity talk about his Samurai history.

Jacqueline turned to Kelly. "What the Fuck was that!?"

Kelly smiled. "Maybe we just don't ask the right questions."

"What the hell do we have here, Kelly? I mean, she is interfacing with the whole shitteree. I mean her view has got to be as vertical as it is horizontal. Her mind is circling back everywhere all the time. I made one suggestion. You heard it, right?"

"Yes."

"Yeah, so I ask her or suggest to her—that we could use a plan. And our Starseed Princess designs a complete set of imagination technologies on the fly.

"I mean—What the Fuck do we have here?"

92

"Why don't we pull back a few light years and try to decide if we are in a God delusion."

That was the first indication Jesus was in the play. He has been head-down, out-of-sight up until now.

"What do you have in mind, now that we're here, Jesus?"

Che was setting up for an argument with Jesus—a zero-respect indication from the jungle fighter.

"I've had a great deal of practice being the Son of God, Che Guevara. You, the man of demoralizing hero worship. Did the Cuban revolution ever help anyone beyond selling hats and T-shirts in your case?"

Laughter begins rolling out of the crowd. Solomon and Muhammad exercising their senior position against the contradictory detail of youth. Che and Jesus are dilettante in the eyes of the old ones. They had been silent most of the trip, but now . . . "*You are both a couple of fakes.*" Their hard looks were now bearing down on the youngsters.

The membrane now positioned and secured, Kelly Marie did an audible, clearing her throat. As all eyes moved to her stratum, she stood.

"Let us thank Solomon and Muhammad for their clear-headed assessment of Che and Jesus. My question is, however, do we feel better because of their comments? This is about ingrained sabotage. The masterly job of eroding confidence with no solutions. No listening. No nothing beyond abuse."

Kelly put her hand to her face and cocked her head toward Merrilee. "What do you think?"

Merrilee cocked her head down and pinched her nose with her right thumb and forefinger. "The opener was a little snarky, but all in all, some real promise, Kelly . . . real promise. So, okay, here is the plan."

Merrilee stands with Kelly's 5H Koh-i-Noor between her teeth.

"We are now synchronous. Individual experiences are shared. I pre-loaded everyone's life experience into a compressed matrix. You are 'One' content node, and I am the server. Machine learning will scan your activity in real time. That will be fed to artificial intelligence (AI) for traits. You will be advised how to proceed."

"No, No, No, Merrilee! Bad idea!" comes ringing out of Jacqueline.

"But, you said . . ."

"I know what I said, but this pushes it too far. We are not ready for this kind of advanced processing. It's really my fault. I had no idea who you were and are. But I am getting that ironed out real fast. Let's you, Kelly Marie, and I have a sit-down over next moves. I have this gnawing epiphany that our God particle guy has no idea what he's up against."

93

There was a shrill noise from the membrane. Sounded like a drill or band saw. Jacqueline had Kelly and Merrilee sequestered in a quiet conversation on a new agenda. But the noise? What was the noise? The three of them stood to see. The membrane was a thermoplastic polymer. So, it reacted to frequency much the same as a speaker reacting to frequency that ends up as music.

Everyone in the membrane was aware of the sound. But the significant awareness rested in Kelly Marie. She jerked around and took Merrilee by the arm.

"That's a Herbig-Haro sound!"

"That's a what?" came from Jacqueline as Kelly abruptly puts her hands against the polymer.

"It's vibrating!" she announces. "It's on the frequency."

When Kelly sat down, she was smiling.

"I'm going to bet our God Particle guy is not what he portrays. I'm going to speculate here, but hear me out. He is the harmonic off the frequency of a developing star. He is a direct biproduct of a Herbig-Haro object. And he doesn't know it. He thinks his existence is made of whole cloth—real but it isn't. This guy is on the spectrum, as we used to say. He is being gaslighted by his own rhetoric. He will disappear and no one will be the wiser. Our reality here is like "New Jeans" jumping off the page at Rolling Stone and then saying 'good night' a billion times toward infinity."

"Wow!" is the unified exclaim from Jacqueline and Merrilee.

Kelly slides off her, there but isn't there, perch to finish her thought.

"So, what we have is a deep space anomaly. The frequency has him thinking he's God. He's not anything. That's why we don't see him. We only hear him. And I will cover my bet with this: The Six-Winged Seraphim hovering around him are trying to figure out how to turn this guy off."

All three start turning their heads like Charlie McCarthy with no Edgar Bergen.

"Then where are we, Kelly? Where are we really?"

"I'm on it and that answer won't take long. But my suggestion is we return to the opening of the original tear in the fabric of space-time and reposition the membrane well away from Nebula. Otherwise, we are going to be chasing weak fields through geodesic metrics forever."

All head swings stopped and nodded in agreement.

Kelly was off to her 5H Koh-i-Noor for new coordinates.

Kelly was back in a hurry.

"Here is where we went wrong. My original calculations did not take into consideration the 'Hubble constant' at 156,000 miles per hour per megaparsec."

The Hubble constant, to make sense, needs conversion factors:
1 kilometer = 0.621371 miles
1 hour = 3600 seconds
Given the Hubble constant is approximately 70 km/s/Mpc, we can calculate it as follows:
70 km/s/Mpc × 0.621371 miles/km × 3600 seconds/ho
Or: 156,000 miles per hour per megaparsec.

"So, we have this 'Lead/Lag' situation. We need to be looking for God like we are a ground-to-air missile system."

Aquinas corrects the thought with *"But God is omnipotent."*

Kelly answers, "Not if we think we have God and, instead, have random harmonics bouncing off the membrane. God may have a path to omnipotence, but God is still a particle mass that positions at will. It's like he shows up for work. Like he drives on omnipotent streets to get somewhere. But I will give you this . . . He drives pretty God-damn fast!"

Everyone laughs as Kelly spins her tale of a Hot Rod God on his way to work.

"So, what's the 'fix', Kelly?" Jacqueline asks, shaking her head like she is trying to sneeze. Then she does sneeze, and the polymer walls shake in a kind of 'Jacqueline harmonic.'

"*That's it! That's it!* Did you all see what just happened? Jacqueline just put a 'Jacqueline harmonic' into a sheet of thermoplastic polymer. God is going to do the same thing if he will just get his track right."

Kelly Marie was on top of her game.

95

"So, what is the 'God Harmonic,' Kelly?"

"I'm going to use Entropy and Twister Geometry for that, Aquinas. In quantum mechanics, states are combined by amplitudes. We have been expecting God to be some kind of omnipotent transparency. I think the reverse is more accurate. God remains on top of the stack in mass density."

"*That can't be. You are describing a singularity leading to the death of a massive star, Kelly! God does not die.*"

"And what is your basis for 'God is forever,' Aquinas?"

"*God is existence in total. Therefore, he is never in dissipation. God is forever.*"

"You do understand, Aquinas, that nothing supports your position in nature?"

Che makes an oblique turn as he asks, from behind Aquinas, "So, what the hell. Are we a First Aid Mission trying to keep God alive?"

The silence erupts everywhere and seems like forever. Raw information has a special way of stopping conversations.

"So, let's figure this out, people. This is beginning to sound like 'Operation Entebbe.' Or maybe 'Neptune Spear.'"

The Art of War's Sun Tzu is picking up the cues that this adventure may not be as it appears.

Kelly gives Merrilee a pleading look. Merrilee doesn't move. Then she looks to Jacqueline. Nothing. Kelly was so far out on a limb the trunk was no longer available.

"Well, isn't this just funny" comes from Jesus Christ, sitting cross-legged in a corner. "Nobody seems to know what's going on."

John's eyes begin changing into their special fallen angel spectrum. "Shut the fuck up, Jesus. This is not your game."

John looks at Merrilee.

96

It's hard to calculate complete silence in deep space. But, John's admonition to Christ had jounce. The reality was setting in that style differences around a table of powerful beings was not to be trifled with.

The lingering question remained on the table.

"Are we caught up in a complex web of deception?"

"Is Merrilee a starseed patriot with a dark agenda? Or is she an ecclesiastic counterpoint to Lucifer?"

"Is Hildegard of Bingen a contrivance of Seraphim propaganda?"

"Is Aquinas nothing beyond a stupid old man in love with his troubadour?"

It was beginning to look like this adventure could be the second coming of the Golden Calf. Who would pick up the sword? Monumental rage would soon be in the pot. Che Guevara, the dashing rebel, was the universal elixir. Everyone watched quietly as Che rose to the occasion.

"I believe in Princess Merrilee. I am willing to follow Jacqueline, anywhere, and I know I will never be as intelligent as Kelly Marie."

It was classic Che. Brilliantly evoked. The sighs of relief were all around. A collective exhale almost gave the membrane an increased pressure gradient.

Jacqueline moved in between Merrilee and Kelly Marie.

"Within our moment in time, Princess Merrilee will be the person who changes the Universe."

With that, John spoke under his breath to Sun Tzu, "Now, I suppose we will have to stand around and marvel at her fucking corona."

Kelly Marie stepped behind Jacqueline and spoke low without vibrations. "So, now can I change the coordinates and get us out of here?"

97

"How critical are your settings, Kelly?"

Jacqueline is keeping to her pace of management style. She never tries to subvert an answer given. She simply calls for clarification, which is how she got to be among the largest business magnets in North America.

"It's not about 'critical' as much as it's about noticing a density change in the fourth dimension of space and time."

Kelly Marie, a top-tier academic scholar, was comfortable with Jacqueline's management style.

"You see, Jacqueline, space-time really doesn't 'tear' as we say in day-to-day vernacular. There is a density change as it warps. There are segments that seem to disappear. That's where we get in. Like we sort of sneak in between the bolt and the striker plate."

"You're amazing, Kelly. Fucking amazing!"

Across the membrane, Merrilee had called for a meeting of everyone, save Kelly, to discuss strategy and open-ended questions. There was a general uneasy silence. People felt secure, but the basis for that security was like being outside the perimeter of a snake strike. Tentative.

Muhammad was the first to speak. *"Merrilee, are you free to discuss your intention?"*

"You mean, do I have a target?"

"Yes, I guess that would be accurate."

"My answer will be scattered. We originally knew that John and Che were bleeding the power frequency of Heaven to ground. Slow but consistent. We did not know that John was Lucifer in the same frame. That was a surprise. However, that situation triggered the possibility that the Almighty Power of Heaven was in some kind of dead short problem.

"At the same time, Hildegard of Bingen was marshaling help to equal out the gender influence of Heaven. She and Aquinas were aware of the power drain. To that end, she met with John in the Suzzallo Library on the University of Washington campus. She came to him in the form of a Raven, warning him of what was to come with an implied suggestion he come along.

"Overlapping this, I was in Pisces below Andromeda with my father, Ra. He was plotting an overthrow of Heaven. The noticeable power drain was his incentive to make a takeover play against the High Holy Order of God. My father was angry due to his loss of significance as the Sun God of Egypt. This was his chance, I guess, to regain his power and influence.

"The problem for me, I was never told of Ra's true intention. He arranged for me to be made hyperpowerful. Through his influence, I was instilled with a Supernova. So, now, I'm floating around as a young woman—in relative terms anyway—with the power amplification of exploding stars. Made no sense to me. That power load was my father's idea to use me as an insurgent against God. He conveniently forgot to tell me that was his plan.

"Not caring much, I go on as Bastet, the protector of women and children in Egypt. But my natural curiosity has me noticing the power drain to John. A mere three and a half million light years away. So, I start following him.

"As the Hildegard of Bingen / Thomas Aquinas plan for change in Heaven develops, I'm watching all of you come together. Aquinas comes to Paris to check out John. John talks Kelly Marie and Jacqueline into joining. The powers in Heaven start staging for another Peloponnesian War, and the enigma of Heaven begins to split. All of you here were on the side of the Zodiac. Unfortunately, we have lost the Scorpion along the way.

"Long story short, I decide to come for a visit. Maybe I can do some good—provide my history and influence. At this point, I have picked up on the 'straighten out God' conversations and I decide to visit Jacqueline and ask her to help me with my approach to the issues. What I forgot, of course, was I am Bastet, a human-sized black cat designed to kill Apep the Snake. My opening moments with Jacqueline are classic Jacqueline—'What the Fuck'—if I may use that phrase in this context.

"Anyway, as a shapeshifter I can be Bastet and Merrilee. We worked that out.

"The big picture overview is that we are looking for God. Not to destroy him but to practice some advice and consent. Our problem, so far, is the lack of benevolence in deep space. The harmonics seem to be obsessed with power, not love.

"Our obvious complication is John as Lucifer. But I have come to believe Lucifer is as interested in stability as we are. Without the yin yang of good and evil, his relevance disappears.

"More questions . . . Yes, Sun Tzu?"

Sun Tzu was a dominant fixture around Princess Merrilee. She anticipated, from the beginning, that a military strategist—no less a general from 800 years before the invention of Christ—would be vital to her success. He was the obvious choice.

Sun Tzu wrote *Sunzi bingfa*, known in Western culture as *The Art of War*. His question in this frame, however, was about Che Guevara and the Samurai.

"Go ahead, Sun Tzu."

"Merrilee, earlier, when you were walking with Kelly Marie and Jacqueline, you broke away to visit Che. My speculation told me that meeting was about his time in Samurai culture."

"You are correct, Sun Tzu."

"Can you tell us more about that meeting and your decisions accordingly."

"Sun Tzu, as a military strategist, you operated among the period of six warring states in China. Around 770 BCE as I recall?"

"That is correct."

"It occurred to me that you were an expert on struggles for supremacy. A person who can develop strategy around six warring factions is unique indeed. But, to answer your question. I wanted a companion discipline. I found that in Che Guevara, but I had to ignite it somehow. That is when I decided to send Jacqueline and Kelly Marie to see Minamoto no Yoshitsune. I knew Che's male subconscious would surface around my decision to send two women. And, of course, we all noticed him begin to practice with his naginata in the wind. So, you see, Sun Tzu, I am not above some friendly strategic moves myself. Sometimes a demonstration in kind is stronger than a command for action."

Sun Tzu smiled and sat down. Merrilee was indeed coming out as 'The Game' strategist. Perhaps a Charlamagne. Her strategic moves demonstrated her understanding of unseen adversaries. If she were to be up against a gang of multilateral gods, she was prepared with Sun Tzu and Che Guevara. If all the decisions became unilateral, she had the personal capacity to move it forward. But that group did not answer the need for the rest as she was about to find out.

"What about us?" enters the conversation with blade precision.

Aquinas. Hildegard, Muhammad and Solomon were not hearing what they needed.

"You, and I say that collectively, are my bedrock Ecclesiastes. At least it's your book, Solomon. You four are the credibility of this entire adventure." '

Merrilee understood the concern, and it was true. She needed their strength of history to make her case to God.

"There is no better quartet, my dears."

This group of words is becoming the bellwether of Merrilee's competence.

Kelly rounds up, revolving her Koh-i-Noor pencil with her tongue.

"We are leaving in T minus Two minutes and fifty-six seconds."

Everyone made a dash for the walls of the membrane.

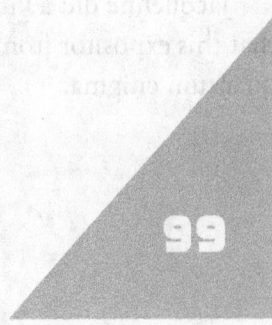

99

"Some people might believe we have 'The Right Stuff' as we appear and reappear in deep space, looking for anomalies in the warp of the fourth dimension."

Kelly, still rolling her pencil between her teeth, remained focused as she spoke. There was a feeling of general well-being on this shot into the black. No nebula vibrating the membrane. The track was clean. In some ways, simply by its precision, it was a threat.

Merrilee had cleaned up the mystery around the mission. They were obviously a cohesive unit, with well-measured plans. Her candor in conversation was a break from her elusive behavior early on. In the Jennet Conant context, everyone became 'The Irregulars.' All selected due to the polish on their experience. The unanimity of a rifle squad standing proud at 'parade rest.'

The membrane speed was accelerating faster than before. The speed of light seemed slow now. They were spinning with time across clear inflationary bubbles at horrific speeds. Everything was different. Nothing was awkward.

"I wonder if we are approaching the Singularity of God?" Kelly speculates in her frolic of explosive neurons. But no one questioned her remark. No one could get close to Kelly's capacity. Physics was an awkward impasse for Kelly Marie. Intelligence beyond all who walked the Earth, her life became narrow at times.

As they went, Jacqueline stood like the Pantheon. Like she was the head of the receiving line for Charles de Gaulle or Napoleon. She was the soldier – statesman – architect, and that called for a genuflect at her door.

Jacqueline did a kind of deep space pivot to Merrilee, understanding that this expositor from another place was the path and the future of the quantum enigma.

100

"What bothers me is—I might be right."

Kelly Marie reminds everyone in a single warning that if they are approaching a singularity—and if they are taken in—that's the end of time for them. It's over. They will never escape.

The immediate overriding question became, "Was God worth the risk?"

After all, their existence was far from perfect, but slamming that existence shut didn't have much appeal either. Having a sit-down with God in fields of green was one thing. Swooping past a singularity into infinite density to find the nothing of the nothing—who needs that?

Was the conformal diagram of a black hole correct? Nobody knew. Passing the singularity would put them in a cosmological horizon of maximal, infinite entropy. Like stuffing sixty trillion eggs into one twelve-egg carton.

Of course, horizons vary. The more one moves, the more the horizon changes. Where, then, is the event horizon of God? It was noteworthy to Jesus Christ that this mix of alive and dead beings were bilaterally not interested in becoming nothing. His rejoinder: "Ha, you're not going to have me to kick around anymore."

John's eyes hardened into the black diamonds of Calcutta—his features fire blue—as he places his own rejoinder on the table . . .

"So much for the field of green."

101

Lucifer is exquisite in a perverse kind of way. It's easier to understand why people find him compelling when he shows his diamond black eyes with fire blue features. But, as he stands, he finds his style stuck in his all-too-often dilemma of mixing conflict and manipulation into confrontation.

In this moment, however... Lucifer knows God can be had. The edge is slight. Their fight was inconclusive. Maybe God just got lucky. Therefore, how to proceed? If Kelly is correct, the gravity will be so intense that light will disappear across the singularity with everything else. Therefore, avoidance would be practical—but no God. The swirling matter around the black is the 'accretion disk' Lucifer has, sometimes hung out in various accretion environments to see if there be a God who might come out for another go. So, he knows they can get that close.

The visual everyone understands is 'spaghettification.' Which means, if they do go in, the first order of business from the hole's perspective is to reduce everyone to a package of Mission Spaghetti, aka Macaroni.

Everyone sees the humor—but not really.

John, being 'Lucifer,' has one more arrow in his quiver. 'Hypothetical Exotic Matter.' Within seconds of John suggesting this last idea, Jacqueline begins to laugh, almost uncontrollably.

"Leave it to John to introduce a plan that begins with the word 'Hypothetical'!"

John smiles. "Leave it to my old escort sex worker to see the humor."

The membrane pivots to as quiet as a black hole is black.

Jacqueline snarls and hits him with. "You arrogant limp-dick motherfucker!" and comes at him with a hammer-sized piece of 3200 bronze.

Solomon and Muhammad look like a couple of oversized fire blankets as they both jump on Jacqueline to quell her fury. In time, Merrilee helps Jacqueline out from under the fire blankets and smiles as she hears Kelly say, "I think Jacqueline would have held the high ground by simply not responding."

Both John and Jacqueline, now smeared with the clutter of anger, go on to consider the merits of 'Hypothetical Exotic Matter.' They were an academic match in social stratification. They both understood hierarchies, including gender, race and class. And they understood that what just happened, if continued, would bring down the mission. In some ways it was good. A demonstration of 'do what I say, not what I do.'

Eventually, John provided enough data to Jacqueline for a command decision. She agreed that using quantum mechanics to produce 'antigravity' could get them through. It was a stretch, but her tone was solid as she announced, "If we are in for a penny, we are in for a pound. We're going in."

102

Anxious to make solid decisions, Kelly Marie pulls a lunchbox size metal case out of her stuff. "Microlensing," she says. "That's how we will spot the specifics."

Kelly Marie was a product of the University of California at Berkeley. Astrophysics was her game. Her plan was to catch the target black hole as it passed in front of a background star. She would capture the light arcing around the density of the target.

Merrilee was hard-focused on the box. "Are you certain, Kelly?"

"Yes, but all our decisions must be made around bending light. It's going to a gravity package I've never used. But Physics is Physics. It's predictable."

"How much time do we have for a shot?" Merrilee is doing some mental calculations.

"Once we have the hole centered, or at least centered in a hexagon abstraction, we will have only minutes to move. This is a constant ready drill, Merrilee. We must be ready all the time."

"Okay, are we self-contained going in? Do we need anything beyond what we have?"

"We could use God . . . just kidding . . ."

Ernie Pyle worked as the managing editor of the *Washington News*. Later, he became a roving journalist for Scripps Howard newspapers. During World War II, he followed American forces through Europe and the South Pacific. In 1945, a sniper's bullet took his life.

Jacqueline was quiet in her thoughts. But she could feel Ernie Pyle. It wasn't going to be just "Brave Men" this time, he said. "The course of women is about to change forever. We are on the dais of women's creative inspiration."

Jacqueline could see herself as Eleanor Roosevelt inviting Merrilee to the White House for afternoon tea. Celebrities flocking outside to see the woman who stopped time—who changed the paradigm of history. If this was fantasy in the critical eye of time, Jacqueline, Kelly Marie, and Merrilee were talking back, as Kelly Marie triangulated a beachhead in the High Holy Order of God.

Merrilee saw herself at the feast of Jericho, then riding into Jerusalem on a colt. The difference: The colt was carrying a light beam rider with the power of twenty thousand suns.

104

Kelly jerked her head up! "Stand By!" "Stand By!" she shouted. As her eyes scanned the monomers of polymer overhead, the outside image was developing into bright star streaks that looked like straws. They were long, like in a time lapse photograph.

"Everybody to the walls!" she shouted. "We are about to reap the wind." Kelly was almost screeching in her voice. A high pitch like the tone before a 'Flat Line.'

Aquinas was still standing. *"How enigmatic. How mysterious."*

"Sit the fuck down, Aquinas!" barks Che as he streaks past with both hands attached to Aquinas's cassock. They stack on each other rolling to the membrane wall.

Kelly's shrill cry was spot on. They were stepping off the curb into the rush of cosmic wind. The particles were shrieking out of control. The 'mysterious' out of Aquinas was a dramatic understatement. The intense gravity was warping the membrane. Now, instead of a loaf, it resembled a gourd. Kelly knew she had the event horizon in her geometry. She was holding on. If there was ever to be a true example of 'Alice' steering a Saturn rocket into 'Wonderland' it was right now.

As they got closer, the warp of space and time was the increasing norm. That distortion changed the visual display. The stars got longer as the sky became the abstract Vincent van-Gogh's "The Starry Night." The shrieking voices and environments became one.

As they crossed the event horizon—beginning the fall—the laws of physics changed. It was like there were no laws of physics. In fact, no laws of anything. The horrific noise went to null. The stretching and torquing from extreme gravity began to backwind.

Sun Tzu looked to Muhammad. *"I feel like we are being rolled out of a rug or something."*

Muhammad, willing to seize the moment, said, *"Well, we have many rugs."*

As people looked around, all their fellows looked like human bananas or cucumbers as they slowly returned to their former shapes.

Jacqueline's voice came over the crowd. "Everyone ok?"

There was a resounding *"Yes!"*

Kelly Marie started to bite her right lower lip . . . looks at Merrilee . . ." "Do ya think we're in?"

Merrilee took a smooth black stone from her fingers over her palm.

"By the grace of Ahura Mazda, Babylonia, Sparda, Arabia and Egypt, we are in."

105

Everyone within earshot was surprised by Merrilee's response to Kelly Marie. But there was little time to discuss that. The membrane was as distorted as its occupants. It looked more like an empty plastic bread bag than the cosmic traveler it was. That would change.

The bright minds were alive and well.

Kelly, looking into her geometry targeting thing, says, "I'm seeing flow lines due to state-vector reductions."

Sun Tzu was having his own look. *"I think these are flow lines due to information loss at the singularity."*

The mentality was like a rifle squad debriefing back from the Ho Chi Minh Trail. Their environment, however, was asking a different question in its sense-data astonishment: *"Do you have any idea where you are!?"*

That was the moment of their reality. *"Do you have any idea where you are?"* And as they looked around for the inquisitor, nobody was there. The actuality of a multiverse—of String Theory; of Hawking's box; and the Hamiltonian Flow—was in their face.

Everyone began moving closer together. Sliding on their bottoms. Not willing to stand making an easy target. Their heads on swivel necks. Their arms pressed close to their chests. Breathing abbreviated but fast. The odd part was that their hemostats were the same. They were no longer segmented as 'alive' and 'dead.' Everybody had a heart rate BPM. Everybody was breathing. And everybody was cold. Then the 'voice' returned like static over a public address horn. Loud, profuse, irritating.

"My dear travelers, we will speak to you in the West Germanic language of the Indo-European language family unless you prefer another," ... the voice continued.

"There are close to 110 astronomical objects in the interstellar catalog. 40 galaxies, 29 globular clusters, 27 open clusters, 6 diffuse nebula, 4 planetary nebulae, and 1 Milky Way patch. The measure varies due to a 500km diameter minimum requirement."

Jacqueline stood. "I am Jacqueline, the expedition leader, representing the intrepid travelers of the vast cosmos. We bring you Princess Merrilee of NGC-234, Pisces, and M31 Andromeda ... in the frame of the standard catalog."

Che lays his head on Aquinas's shoulder. They were still sort of entangled from their toss to the membrane wall.

"Wow, Jacqueline just grabbed that donkey by the tail!"

Aquinas puts his fingers to Che's lips, in a careful and gentle manner. *"Listen, I think there is about to be a lot more."*

"My dear Jacqueline, and to your charge, you have ascended the limits of your existence. You have crossed the celestial boundary—the horizon of time. You are that of no other Being. Never has the celestial symphony of souls seen such a blur in the structure of pure light."

Jacqueline turned to Merrilee and extended her hand of introduction.

Merrilee acknowledged Jacqueline as she stood. The space around Merrilee seemed to resonate; undulating like a full-spectrum aurora.

"You are Merrilee?" the horn voice inquired. All its sound scratchiness gone.

"I am."

There was a bounce—like someone dropped a microphone. Then an advance exhale. Still no visual. Then a cleared throat ... in breathtaking mystery ...

"I am Michael, the Archangel."

106

Merrilee stood quietly before she spoke again. Long enough to keep the situation ill-at-ease. She began.

"You are the great captain of the Heavenly Hosts. A warrior defending against the attack of evil. You were God's word speaking to Moses on Mount Sinai. You are the one who holds the secret of God's Creation of Heaven and Earth."

"As it is written," comes from the Archangel. Merrilee continues.

"Your original feast in Phrygia is September. I share that time with you. You, the Archangel Warrior and Protector of God. I am the Galactic Protector of women and children. We share power as Emperor Seraphim. You hold the power of the sword, Michael the Archangel, and I am the Dragon you have yet to meet."

Jacqueline faces everyone with a twisted smile. "Well, who knew our first hour in Heaven could roll downhill this fast!"

Aquinas and Hildegard agree between themselves, and signal Jacqueline, "*Merrilee is at the door of the Apocalypse in the Book of Revelation.*"

The provocative rejoinders from Merrilee triggered a manifestation of Michael the Archangel in a spectacular flash of fragments. Merrilee wasted no time notifying The Archangel of their roughly equal mass. Unimpressed with the Heavenly pyrotechnics, Princess Merrilee had positioned herself four-square at the table of the High Holy Order.

107

The capacious format of Heaven wasn't lost on anyone sitting on their hands waiting for Merrilee to level a Hyperstrike at the Archangel. The Seraphim of Heaven had lots of wiggle room in a fight, their arena being infinite. But Merrilee demonstrated that she was not risk-averse. She went for the Archangel's emotional jugular in the opening moments, and she got what she wanted.

When in Egypt riding the night sky with Ra, Merrilee, as Bastet, operated like a member of a wolf pack. She rode with her head under her father's chin. When Apep the snake threatened, Ra appeared as a God with two heads. Formidable indeed. Wolvess operate the same way in tight pairs. Nature has a way of being habitual.

What the Archangel knew, instinctively, was that Merrilee would be the second head to anyone in her wolf pack. There was no off-script back story here. Merilee did not come to play. She came to win. Aquinas and company were bewildered by her strategic moves—and her obvious power. In the past, she seemed to be an accidental success. In this encounter with the Archangel, Merrilee was an arsenal of equivalency.

Merrilee's power and positioning, heretofore mostly unsung, was a mixed blessing for the group. They were immediately suspected in their every action. They were instantly front-line adversaries in the whiffing delicacy of Heaven.

108

"Might I remind Princess Merrilee that she is at the seat of unrestrained energy and power. That although her capacity for parlay is on full display, her impressive triumph over the Archangel remains an eroding paradox of circumstance." Aquinas opened abruptly in contrast to his Angelic Doctor persona—sounding more laity than cleric. Aquinas, the most celebrated cleric in history, was not a convenient synopsis of religious tradition. Merrilee took notice of his observations and suggested he join her with his 'Five Proofs' of God when next the Archangel might appear. He agreed.

Without the emerging Archangel, the environment was noticeable. Breathtakingly vibrant in a clean tranquility of blue. As ethereal as it should be in their interstellar synapse of wonder. The horizon seamless to the Euclidian plane. If celestial light was a thing, they were standing in it.

With divine harmony, yet no divine. To the writers among them, Hildegard and Aquinas, this was the Author's Preface. The 'take off your shoes' anteroom to the fashion, faith, and fantasy of existence.

In the land of too many variables, the significance of one can be hard to grasp. The yin yang of power can go hopelessly wrong. If this God of gods is 'all knowing,' did he know that the assassination of Austrian Archduke Franz Ferdinand would precipitate the death of sixteen million people? Did he know of the Nazis? Or Holodomor? Or Cambodia? Or Rwanda? Or Dzungar? Or Bangladesh? Or Genghis Khan?

And if he did, Merrilee and company are not at the seat of benevolence and power. They are at the seat of death, incompetence and corruption.

109

"I think what we have here is the actuality of Aristotle's second book of ethics regarding proper function."

This sounded odd coming from Che Guevara, especially considering it was Aquinas who liked Aristotle. Regardless, his point was valid as he continued . . .

"No one has been able to demonstrate the good, or the evil, of God. There are trillions of confabulations in thought, but nothing in fact. People who claim 'fact' and become defensive are in an erotomania delusion. God has no obligation for fidelity to the faithful. And the reverse is true.

"Aquinas, better than anyone, understood this. Which is probably why he continued concentrating on "Proof of God' until the end of his life. And, only in the last two years of his life on Earth did he manage to produce his final conclusions in *Summa Theologica*. Even Aquinas was never certain God existed. He hoped, as did the many.

"To this there are no exceptions. And that being the most ratifiable reason why we are sitting in the anteroom of God in this Alice in Wonderland moment. Who is behind the curtain?"

Sun Tzu motioned to Che. *"That speech sounds to me like you had a lot of time in the jungles of Bolivia to think about your fate left to myth. The good news, Che, is we are having a conversation with the Archangel. And that does make a direct tie to the Trinity of the High Holy Order. And we appear to be the first contingency of human beings to make it this far as inquisitors."*

"So, what about this, Sun Tzu?"

Kelly Marie mapping on Che and Sun Tzu the question about the new set of hemostasis applied to everyone in the party—dead or alive. "What about that?"

Sun Tzu takes it forward.

"My guess is people who die in the cosmos go into the outer dimensions as might be the original plan. We, on the other hand, just showed up. And that is a first for everyone involved, including the Archangel and God and, and . . . So, I think we are all alive once again. We are out of context in the eyes of the High Holy Order.

"In the face of the situation, they circle us back to zero—make us all alive and we begin again."

"Wow! Sun Tzu!" as Kelly Marie looks around for support. "That's amazing!"

But Lucifer puts it in a human context as he pivots to Aquinas.

"Aquinas, I cannot believe I am going to have to deal with an old fucker like you all over again."

Everyone begins to laugh.

Then it occurs to the few the Change. That the overhead sky isn't sky. It's Michael the Archangel extending a set of shimmering gold and silver wings over the crowd. He is just there. Like, "Right there!" as Hildegard puts the situation in their setting.

Michael has revealed himself in this almost preschool scare appearance. He is quiet; looking around. He's sitting on a mountainside. There is no context for size. Sometimes he is as big as the mountain. Sometimes he is small. Like a bird airing out wet wings at the end of a mud trail. He doesn't seem to expect devotion. Looking at him brings an overwhelming sense of peace. There was light, but it was inspiring light. Not intense light. It was full-spectrum light broken down. Not white. It was blue and yellow and red and all variants in between.

He looked like a warrior, leather belt, chest armor, long sword, sandals. He was sort of silver and bronze. His wings, silver and gold. When he looked large, like the mountain, and he rotated his wings, that just scared the shit out of everyone. Then he spoke . . .

"You have something deeply hidden."

Everyone immediately looked at Merrilee—everyone!

The Archangel draped his wings. "You are Princess Merrilee?"

"I am."

"I only heard your voice earlier. Now I see you. I know you from Mount Olympus."

"And I know you, Archangel."

"We are happy you answered our call, Princess Merrilee."

"None of my group know you called me, Archangel."

110

Hildegard of Bingen looks at Jacqueline and speculates, "Do you suppose we are at Domrémy Bar, France, and Princess Merrilee is a manifestation of Joan of Arc. Do you suppose that all the Micheal the Archangel business is simply a holographic re-creation of Joan of Arc's relationship with the Archangel? . . . this is history, not speculation."

Jacqueline, being the leader she was, does some quick history calculations.

"You are right on a couple of counts, Hildegard. Merrilee's time as Bastet, with Ra, gave her lessons in double agency and as we stand here today, she is having this 'we sent for you' conversation with the Archangel. And it was Michael the Archangel, the most powerful Seraphim ever, who mentored Saint Joan of Arc.

"If you're right, we're in great shape, and it makes sense that we don't know Merrilee's full story. She had lots of practice by example at the French advance against the fort des Tourelles leading to the French victory at Orléans. I don't want to perseverate, Hildegard, but she was an armor-clad woman who led an army of men to national victory."

Aquinas, disbelieving, blinked. *"How do you get Divine Guidance from a woman who goes to war?"*

He and Kelly Marie are staring at each other.

"There is much to this than we've been let in on, Kelly."

"I get the obvious, Aquinas, but look at our mix. What is it about us that drives Merrilee and the Archangel to enter a secret mission, and bring us along?"

Jacqueline laughs her way into the conversation again. "I think we are with her now because she's been here before."

"How so, Jacqueline?"

"If this shapes up to be between good and evil, or just plain misuse of power in Heaven, there is going to be conflict—maybe a trial, could be a war. Merrilee is endowed with courage. We see that every day. And she's not stupid. Look at the talent base we represent. Even Lucifer has some self-interest in this pack. Look at Jesus Christ over there in the corner. Do you think he could use a little boost?

"Merrilee has arranged us as a win for everyone. Michael the Archangel knows her and knows her power. That's why he called. He has an agenda. Maybe she owes him. Maybe she trusts him. I don't know, but we will find out soon. So, we are the Court of Merrilee walking into the castle with a heroine as her Royal Court collaborators. The big difference with this is none of us were born to the court. 'We Are Who We Are'—to sort of parrot René Descartes to the Queen. We sit behind our Princess/Queen, the one with the power of twenty thousand suns—and nobody fucks with us.

III

As Michael the Archangel and Princess Merrilee commiserate over old times on Mount Olympus, her membrane group speculates on the Court Life of Heaven. Kelly Marie has an enormous sense of accomplishment for it appears she placed the membrane at God's front door. Aquinas remains as stubborn as a Forest Service mule over the value of *Summa Theologica*. Hildegard of Bingen collars Che Guevara, reminding him that this mission is about gender bias not some tryst between two seraphs off Mount Olympus. Solomon and Muhammad just look around and smile, then laugh.

However, it's Lucifer, as the walk-around man for an invented Jesus Christ who feels the acute nature of every decision going forward. For all the puffery around the reunion of Merrilee and Michael, Lucifer is the only one present who can manifest the power to launch a valid strike against God.

Fully sensing his position, Sun Tzu engages Lucifer with a few years of what Plato had to say about Achilles and Diogenes playing in Zeno's paradoxes.

But it's Jacqueline who understands how everyone could be playing in atoms of emptiness. Her overriding question: "How could a constantly changing Universe continually capture its structure without being an illusion?"

She adds, "How does nothing become a place? I fully understand that Einstein proved out the Atoms of Existence, but he did not establish them as clusters into solids."

"So, here we now sit in a Jacqueline paradox," answers Muhammad, with acquiescence from Solomon who questions the concept. *"Is anything expected? Is time real? Why is laughter associated with funny?"*

Michael the Archangel turns to everyone: "Do not believe that pricking the pomposity of the ruling class will get you any light in your cave. God is an ongoing dialogue with nature. Plato asked the same questions of reality. He failed."

"Well, well, that remark establishes who has the 'pomposity' around here!"

Kelly Marie remained the egalitarian in the group, and she gave no quarter to a political system ruled by allegory. True to her position she put down a marker.

"Why don't you two decide how to solve your endowed reason and tell the rest of us what the hell is going on!"

112

The Archangel was first to apologize for his entrenched hubris.

"I'm off my marks, here. I forgot the risk that fell upon you. The time. The displacement. The milestone decisions kept from you. Please accept my chagrin, but try and understand, you are the most important group in the history of time."

Merrilee followed Michael with her acquiescence of the deals, danger and destiny of everyone.

"All of you remember the frequency drawdown that caused Aquinas to find John. The very person he had sold to Lucifer as his bargaining chip earlier in this timeline. That was the first occasion of concerted action associated with this mission. The High Holy Order was in trouble with its frequency of power, migrating to John as a conductor. Complicating that was Aquinas's priori sale of John that caused him to become an unwitting double of evil—Lucifer.

"This drawdown became the heretofore unimaginable case of the power of God being siphoned off to the Devil. My signal from the Archangel was overlapping in sinewave, but it was evident—for real."

A cursory overview revealed that the power of the high echelon was quickly losing the ability to codify order. The magnitude of what Merrilee and Michael were advancing had everyone locked on the message. Everything seemed on the line. The value of the mind of man. Of existentialism, ethics, stoicism, idealism, rationalism, pragmatism, aesthetics, and metaphysics—all in possible disarray. Even the circumstances around the collapse of Mars may have a connection to frequency.

The Archangel continued, "Even though I have access to God, I am not without fear."

Hearing those words, Aquinas began to quiver. *"Oh, Dear God, I was right all along."*

Hildegard took his hand. "Well, Aquinas, Doctor Angelicus, San Tommaso D'Aquino, you are the most important theologian of the forever and ever, after all."

He smiled. *"There is finally a path, Hildegard. There is a path."*

Sun Tzu was more circumspect. *"If I may be so bold, this conversation sounds like the King of the Franks has decided to have the Saxons over for dinner. Your reverence for God leaves out that he has the high ground. We sit in a cluster speculating on his loss of power. Does anyone know what that means?"*

Che Guevara agrees. "We could be the broken sword of the Samurai."

113

"This may seem invasive, however my relationship with Princess Merrilee, as you now know, dates to Mt. Olympus. As I observed her acute operational style on the mountain, I realized that any revolutionary movement in Heaven must be based on spectacular change. In that, it must be conspicuous to the Universe. The change must provide opportunity and emotional stability. Untold riches as motivation only works with Lucifer—not with spirituality—the drawdown situation notwithstanding."

Jacqueline never has a problem setting the tone for a conversation.

"We are all here riding on distortions of better judgment, Archangel. If I wanted social self-advancement, I should be taking care of business in Vancouver. But NO! I'm sucked into this daisy chain of deception around the frequency of God."

As Jacqueline perpetuated her skepticism, Merrilee asks, "Jacqueline, do you trust me?"

"No!"

Sun Tzu chuckled. *"Well, we are finally getting to the Eisenhower and Montgomery version of the Second World War. Let's remember that what kept them together was the desire for change. We are in the same circumstance now. What Jacqueline and Merrilee think of each other is not as important as how well they work together. And if history serves me, that formula worked out rather well in 1945."*

"Nice try, Sun Tzu, but here is the other problem with Merrilee. Just about the time I will need her most, she will turn into a lion-sized black cat, switch her tail, and bite my arm. Of which I have the Helena emergency room bills and scars to show."

Kelly Marie blinked in disbelief.

"Give it a rest, Jacqueline. Everybody knows you are the apex of strategy on Earth. And, if Merrilee shifts to a Cat, I will talk her down. And I, also, have the experience to show."

Everyone returned to their make-ready tasks as Jacqueline and Merrilee and Kelly Marie finished their first management meeting on the public dais. Most returned with sputters of tactful coughing.

"So, what is your strategy, Jacqueline?"

"God is going to see Merrilee's first appearance as adversarial."

Having listened to the dais exchange, the Archangel decided to fish for some direction from his Earthwise companions.

"A simple, fabulous opportunity . . . we are going to sell God on this one-time option to save the Kingdom of Heaven from drawdown. We have an easy solution to his problem, with one small caveat. He steps down and Merrilee steps up."

"Oh, fuck yes. No problem, Jacqueline!"

Michael the Archangel suddenly becomes the alpha male.

"Who the hell are you, anyway. The Queen of Gaslighting?"

"Try another question, Michael." Jacqueline lays her 'marker' on the table.

Jacqueline's answer conveyed her alpha male assertiveness. She had the Archangel on the run. He knew it, and so did she. Michael's unrepairable defect was his lack of celebrity. He was forever stuck in service to an external cause—God. His call for Merrilee was based on his own insecurity. Michael was a permanent misfit.

"Jacqueline, how can you even imagine God sitting still for such a proposal?"

"That was not about God, Michael. That was about me gauging your reaction. So, tell me Michael the Archangel, what do you expect out of our being here?"

"I DON'T KNOW. I don't know, Jacqueline! The whole place is in disarray. God is surrounded by power-hungry Seraphim. God swivels around like the last acts of *King Lear*. I knew Merrilee from Mt. Olympus. She was smart. She was powerful. She was measured. She was the fulfillment of success. And that is what Heaven needs. God's power is collapsing. His acceptance of that is nowhere to be found. I fear God is going mad. I fear this absurdity will take us all down.

"Well, as bizarre as that seems, I will speak with Merrilee. However, from what you portray, I think we just show up with you in hand and see how he reacts. No threat. Just visitors you know from history. And if God takes a swing at Merrilee, I guarantee you it will be the last swing he ever takes. But that's not Merrilee's style, so let's just open with God's natural reaction."

Then, Jacqueline gives a somewhat guarded report to everyone with, "Okay gang, we are going in as friends of the Archangel. Curious visitors, maybe. Maybe have God show us around. And then we wing it."

Kelly Marie side-eyes Merrilee. *"Wing it?* Is that her rubric for 'I know what I'm doing'?"

Merrilee laughs aloud. "Well, it was Jacqueline who said, 'In for a penny, in for a pound.'"

"Yes, Merrilee, I get that there is some element of risk. But why don't you tell us more about Michael; this fascinating friend you have? Are the two of you wrapped up in some kind of understanding from the past? Do you owe him?"

Merrilee treated the question by grasping the thought.

"No, no. Nothing like that, Kelly. All the Gods of Mt. Olympus operate under a code of cooperation."

Kelly Marie did an immediate 'Kelly Marie.'

"Wait a minute, Merrilee. You just said, *'All the Gods.'* But when we were at Mt. Olympus, you answered a question with *'Yes, I walk with the Gods.'* So, are you an actual 'God?"

"Yeah, pretty much."

"Okay everyone, Michael is going to give us a little heads-up on God before we go in."

Jacqueline steps aside as Michael begins:

"God enjoys burnt offerings so I will provide each of you with a small handwoven candle of sage. You will light it with the starter provided as you enter and pass by the Beersheba. That will be on your right. You are not to look at that altar, as it's God's favorite and he maintains the Beersheba for his own looking.

"One of you must bring a male animal. For example, a bull, lamb, or maybe a goat. This animal must be without blemish, and it will be sacrificed at the door of the temple where God will accept the offering and mix the ashes with salt and honey, which will be served honoring your station as non-Levitical servants."

Solomon gazed in bewildered surprise, then spoke . . .

"'Non-Levitical' indeed! It may interest you, Archangel, that the Crusader army in 1099 and Templar churches in Europe imitated my design."

Che looks at Aquinas. "Is this serious?"

"I think so."

"Next, each of you will announce who you are by name and assume a position on your knees where you will tell God of your faults. God will give you pieces of unleavened cakes as he recites your absolution. At this point you will be considered 'clean' and worthy of his presence. God will then take a ritual bath of 'moral attribute' so you can gaze upon him.

"A large door will open, and Priests, Prophets, and Kings will enter the room from every age, and chant to God that he is 'The Colossal God above Lions.' God will then sit upon a golden throne as winged women fan him as they recite from 'Freedom from the Burden of Judgment,' the most recent codices approved by God himself."

Merrilee and Jacqueline are now standing together, as Jacqueline inquires of the Archangel, "This stuff doesn't seem unusual to you, Michael?"

Michael looks over the group. "It is understandable if we consider the deteriorating mind of 'King Lear'."

All the heads quietly agree.

Then Merrilee looks to the Archangel, "You probably should have asked for help earlier."

As the doors began to open, it was obvious this place was built of parallel tangent vectors around infinite circles. It seemed like every particle of mass had a different address in the creation of universal physics. Entirety in unison. There was a slight odor of fresh flowers. There was a light breeze. There was an element of unknown adventure. There were fashionable attempts to dress, but to no code or style. There was an Escher circle-looking horizon occupied by billions of golden Seraphim.

The dominant feature was a set of stairs leading to iconic columns supporting a pitch roof of marble at the top. It seemed like hundreds of feet. Looked like sandstone and marble. The architecture Greek. It was like someone put the Parthenon on top of infinite stairs. The feeling of Zeno's paradox. No matter how many steps, there was no top, yet it was right there. Marble dionysus pentelikon covering polished façades.

God had set himself up to be a medieval vassal king. The kind of king who gave himself infinite authority of rule beyond the naked eye. What one saw was symbolic power. What one didn't see was the 'Sierpiński Triangle.' That part of Creation that was, in fact, infinite.

The group walked in a slow column, avoiding eye contact with artifacts of interest. It was like nobody wanted to make a wrong move. Michael moved among them. He was quiet, sometimes adjusting a wing; sometimes a squeak or pop in the shift of his armor. Aquinas carried an abridged version of *Summa Theologica* under one arm; his rosary over the other. Sun Tzu carried *The Art of War*. Che carried his *Motorcycle Diaries*. All the men seemed to need icons for support. The women didn't.

Michael worked his way to the front, moving his hand back, palm down, as a signal to move quietly and slowly. He acted like a guide on the African Serengeti. Any moment his charges would experience the magic of a lion under the acacia trees.

117

The Archangel stopped. Stood up taller. Then turned to Jacqueline.

"He's with someone. Listen—just listen carefully. Do you hear him?"

"Yes. Yes, we do!"

"He is listening to someone."

There was a large arc of stars forming high above them, all facing toward where he was. The conversation was quiet but audible.

"Holy Spirit, she's coming. You do understand that?"

"Why are you telling me this, Scorpius?"

Lucifer spun toward Jacqueline. *"FUCK!"*

Jacqueline smiled decisively. Turned to Kelly and winked.

"Be quiet! Just be still. Please!" Michael was obviously uneasy with Lucifer's eruption.

The Scorpion was table-talking with God. There was something wonderfully reminiscent about what everyone could hear. His rumbling trochanters. The tarsus clicks. Just his presence once again.

Lucifer's fear was not without cause. If the Scorpion and God were somehow cohesive, Lucifer had no chance of his own power grab. The shrieking lightning power of the Scorpion would tip any measure away from Lucifer.

The conversation between the Scorpion and God did not linger.

"I'm telling you this, Holy Spirit, because I am aware of her of her fellows. They were close to me, I to them. Their evolution to now has been long. Your top Centurion Guard, Michael the Archangel, called for Princess Merrilee out of fear for you. For the drawdown of power."

"My dear Scorpius, my power might be waning, but that is a far cry from collapse."

"My fear, Holy Spirit, is that the situation will catch you unaware. We cannot afford God to end up the Wizard of Oz. Who you are, we know. What you are must be transparent to the Universe."

Kelly Marie whispers, "How does the Scorpion know this stuff, Jacqueline?"

Jacqueline whispers back:

"I figure he's been talking to The Archangel. From what I'm hearing, Scorpius knows we're here. Probably from Michael. He's just trying to ease God into the actuality of us not being Barbarians at his gate."

"So, they are here, you say, Scorpius?"

"Yes, Holy Spirit. They are here."

118

God quickly moves the conversation to his court's tradition, "Do they bring an offering? Have they passed the doors? Did anyone look at the Beersheba?"

"Where are their offerings?"

God was exercised over his traditions in Heaven.

The Scorpion moved close to God.

"Holy Spirit, the delegation of, and with, Princess Merrilee are contemporaries of power. Princess Merrilee is from the Sun God of Egypt. She is the protector of all women and children. She enjoys the largest temple in the Republic of Egypt. From the northeast corner of Africa and the Sinai Peninsula. The Red Sea. Sudan. Libya. The Gulf of Aqaba in the northeast. From Alexandria, my dear Holy Spirit. She is from the highest level of academics in the Library of Alexandria. She occupies her position at NGC-234 and runs with Andromeda at M31."

God is stunned by the Scorpion's description.

"What say ye, Scorpius? What have you done? Am I cast into your sea of contrivance?"

"No, no, Holy Spirit. I want you to know that offerings are not customary for contemporaries of the High Holy Order."

"My 'contemporary,' Scorpius?"

"Yes, Holy Spirit. Your contemporary."

119

Michael moved forward. He caught the attention of the Scorpion. God turned, looking at Michael.

"You are the one trying to save me, Michael?"

"Yes, Holy Spirit."

"You are the one who is telling the Scorpion I need help?"

"Yes, Holy Spirit."

"Why did you come into my house, Michael? To defy me?"

"No, Holy Spirit."

"I can say, exactly, Archangel. You have destroyed my confidence in you and your tribe of Seraphim."

Michael bends at the waist, "You are my Emperor God of gods."

As Jacqueline listens to the exchange, she remarks, "This sounds like a chess match between non-ranked players. They understand the board but have no understanding of positions or strategy."

Then she turns to Merrilee, "I think it's time for you to step to the plate."

Merrilee, by now, is as one with her traveling team. She makes her way out toward the bent-over Archangel. She walks into the open and stands looking directly at God. Suddenly realizing her location, 60 billion years of history hit her. She breaks into shivers, her very Being goes to dead short. She is speechless.

"And you are? comes ringing down from God.

120

Jacqueline looks back to Kelly Marie, "I think she's choking."

God asks again, *"And you are?"*

Kelly Marie, remembering how Merrilee pulled her out of harm's way multiple times, begins walking forward. Kelly reports, "She is Princess Merrilee from NGC-234."

As she walks, she continues, "You, Mr. God, create stuff. She is the stuff! So, here is the difference. As you create there is no blowback for your creations. You are removed. Like a research scientist. In Merrilee's case, she has been infused with a Super Nova.

"Let's put this another way, Mr. God. If you were standing in a white lab jacket, your glasses on your nose, looking into a test tube for results, you would have no direct involvement in the fusion of your experiment. Merrilee, however, is the stuff in the tube. And if she doesn't like how your glasses sit on your nose, she will explode, blowing you into a parallel universe."

Aquinas is jacking his head in every direction.

"Somebody has got to calm her down. Stop Kelly from referring to the Holy Spirit as 'Mr. God!'"

Merrilee begins to laugh as she puts her hand on Kelly Marie's shoulder, "Who knew this is how I would meet God!" They both grin and laugh and cry together in a solid memory embrace.

God—the Holy Spirit—has never been subjected to such powers of confidence. Now he is laughing. Michael the Archangel is coughing and exhaling in profound relief.

God stops, looks at Merrilee, "And you are . . . the most powerful example of all my Creations!

"Welcome to Heaven, Princess Merrilee!"

THE END

Epilogue

But amidst the weight of revelation, Princess Merrilee of Solana did not waver. The cosmos had always whispered to her— an unbroken voice, a path carved in light. Her triumph was not in conquest, nor in defiance, but in the quiet, undeniable truth that had guided her from the beginning.

*She did not seek to harness divinity.
She sought only to be with God.*

And in that moment, as the stars bled their golden hymn across the expanse, she was.

About the Author

John LaCasse's life has has been filled with almost every conceivable emotion as his adventurous spirit, ongoing curiosity, devil-may-care attitude, and endless love of nature, music, art, animals, friends and family are open, evident and expressed at a moment's notice. Gratitude for loving parents and a grandmother who introduced him to all of the above; pride in business success; anger witnessing betrayal; both joy and grief in fatherhood; love for devoted partners. If "variety is the spice of life," Dr. John LaCasse has consumed multi-milligrams and attracted followers from every walk of life, every age, every gender.

Along the way there have been times to slow down, look around, peek *inside* to see what should be changed and as a result education made a U-turn in middle age and Transcendental learning and teaching, an MBA in International Business, and a Ph.D. at North Central University took precedence. A Forbes School of Business Faculty Member of the Year award echoed the dozens of kudos from his students.

Memberships in the American Association of University Professors, academic honorariums in Kappa Delta Pi and Golden Key, and an examiner for the International Baccalaureate continue his involvement in education, but creative writing has become a passion with now five books in print, including *Fight for the Quantum*, *After Your Children Die*, and *Deals, Danger, Destiny*, the forerunner of *Floppy Feathers*, and *The Hunters*.

John lives in Seattle, Washington, with his life partner, Christine Burgoyne.